UNFORBIDDEN
SWEETS

BOOKS BY JEAN ANDERSON:

The Art of American Indian Cooking (with Yeffe Kimball)
Food Is More Than Cooking
Henry the Navigator, Prince of Portugal
The Haunting of America
The Family Circle Cookbook (with the Food Editors of Family Circle)
The Doubleday Cookbook (with Elaine Hanna)*
Recipes from America's Restored Villages
The Green Thumb Preserving Guide
The Grass Roots Cookbook
Jean Anderson's Processor Cooking
Half a Can of Tomato Paste and Other Culinary Dilemmas (with Ruth Buchan)**
Jean Anderson Cooks

*Winner of the R.T. French Tastemaker Award, Best Basic Cookbook and Best Overall Cookbook of the Year (1975)
**Winner of the R.T. French Tastemaker Award, Best Specialty Cookbook of the Year (1980)

UNFORBIDDEN SWEETS

More Than 100 Classic Desserts You Can Now Enjoy— Without Counting Calories

Jean Anderson

ARBOR HOUSE NEW YORK

For every dieter who dreams of forbidden desserts

ACKNOWLEDGMENTS

I should like to thank Sara Moulton and Mary Higgins for helping me with recipe development and inspiration, and Diane Hodges for the expert manuscript typing.

CONTENTS

INTRODUCTION

Calorie-counters, take heart! There *is* a way to diet and have your cake, too—sinfully rich chocolate cake, frozen raspberry meringue torte, cream puffs, silky avocado ice cream and fresh-baked lemon pie topped by a cloud of meringue.

Impossible, you say? Not at all, because I've subtracted the bulk of the calories from some 120 of the world's most seductive desserts without sacrificing an ounce of their original goodness.

Answered prayers, I think, for the one-in-three Americans who is presently overweight and cannot stick to a diet. Let's face it—those of us who like to eat and have a weight problem (and I consider myself one of that number) *like* our sweets. We feel deprived—*punished*—whenever we must diet. Indeed, we tend to starve ourselves for two weeks only to reward ourselves with a piece of cake at the end. Meaning, of course, that we fall off our diets with a bang, backslide until our consciences get the better of us, then plunge into yet another strict regimen.

The starve-binge system of dieting doesn't work, as too many of us have already learned. Moreover, it can be dangerous. The only successful way to diet is merely to curtail one's calorie intake sensibly—forever, if need be, to eat well-balanced meals (only less at each one).

Sensible dieting, however, need not mean banishing all desserts from our diets. Or confining them to a pineapple ring here and a peach half there. Those of us afflicted with a sweet tooth aren't going to be happy with that kind of dessert. We dream of ice cream and cake.

How wonderful it would be, I thought, to salve my sweet tooth *as* I dieted—with a clear conscience. Was it possible? Could I figure out a way to subtract calories from my favorite desserts? Food, after all, was my profession. And food research my college major at Cornell.

So I went to work decalorizing dozens of the desserts dieters consider off limits—pies and pastries, puddings and mousses, ice creams, cakes and cookies. And I lost 15 pounds in the bargain.

These low-calorie desserts, I found, satisfied me in a way that no "dietetic" dessert ever had. They *tasted* like dessert, rich as all get-out. And yet most of them weigh in at considerably less than 200 calories per serving; a few of them contain less than 100 calories per serving; and none even approaches the 275 per serving generally considered to be low calorie for a dessert (this, by the way, is about the calorie count of a cup of berry yogurt).

Once I got the hang of decalorizing desserts, it all went smoothly. I began by minimizing (and in many instances, eliminating) butter and cream from recipes (yogurt, buttermilk, evaporated skim milk and tofu, I discovered, made marvelously creamy, low-calorie substitutes). For thickening puddings and fillings, for adding body to soufflés, I substituted cornstarch for flour (it contains approximately the same number of calories as flour but has twice the thickening power, meaning you only need to use half as much). I also made the most of the buoyancy of beaten egg whites, the stabilizing ability of plain gelatin and the natural sugars of fresh fruits.

Finally, I've capitalized on the new breakthrough low-calorie sweetener, aspartame, now going "national" in supermarkets under the brand name Equal. It is a wholly new kind of sweetener that has none of the bitter aftertaste of saccharin. Aspartame is synthesized from two common amino acids, the building blocks of protein, that occur naturally in more than half of nature's food. It is 200 times sweeter than sugar, yet a 1-gram packet of granules (the best form for cooking, by the way, because the granules can be mixed with dry ingredients, also because they dissolve almost on contact with liquids) contains just 4 calories. Aspartame's chemical and physical properties, to be sure, are totally unlike those of sugar; thus it cannot be used in place of sugar in baking, in making syrups and cooked frostings, etc. Indeed, aspartame appears to lose some of its sweetness as it is heated. No matter. I've worked out recipes that minimize this revolutionary new sweetener's shortcomings and maximize its plusses, not least of which is that it tastes very much like sugar. But enough scientific talk.

Here, then, are 120 new desserts (each with calorie counts per serving) that are every dieter's fantasy: sensual . . . sumptuous . . . and blissfully low calorie.

Do I dare call them "just desserts"?

Jean Anderson

New York, 1982

1
PIES AND PASTRIES

CRANBERRY-GLAZED OPEN-FACE APPLE TART
Serves 8

An uncommonly good pie that averages only a few calories more per serving than a large apple.

Crust:

>   1 generous spraying of nonstick vegetable cooking spray
>   10 vanilla wafers, rolled to fine crumbs

Filling:

>   4 large Golden Delicious apples, peeled, cored and sliced thin
>   2 tablespoons lemon juice
>   ¾ cup evaporated skim milk
>   1 large egg, lightly beaten
>   1 tablespoon raw sugar
>   Pinch ground cinnamon
>   Pinch ground nutmeg
>   ¼ teaspoon almond extract

Glaze:

>   1 recipe Natural Fruit Glaze (see p. 180)

For the Crust: Spray the bottom and sides of a 9″ pie pan with the nonstick vegetable cooking spray, dump in the vanilla-wafer crumbs, then tilt the pan from one side to another until bottom and sides are lightly but evenly coated with crumbs; spread any loose crumbs evenly over the pan bottom. Set aside while you prepare the filling.

For the Filling: Place apples in a shallow bowl, sprinkle lemon juice evenly over all, then toss very lightly to mix. Arrange the apples in the crumb crust, reserving the prettiest slices for the top layer and arranging them in a sunburst pattern. Beat together all remaining filling ingredients and pour evenly over the apples. Cover the pie with aluminum foil and bake in a moderately hot oven (375°F.) for 20 minutes. Uncover the pie and bake 20 to 25 minutes longer, just until juices bubble and apple slices are touched with brown.

Meanwhile, prepare the Natural Fruit Glaze as recipe directs. Remove the pie from oven, let stand 15 minutes at room temperature, then spoon the glaze evenly over the surface.

Cool the pie to room temperature, cut into 8 wedges and serve. 101 calories per serving.

OPEN-FACE DUTCH PEAR PIE
Serves 8

I doubt that any dinner guest would dream that this rich pie is actually low in calories.

Crust:

1 recipe Pared-Down Piecrust (see p. 51)

Filling:

3 tablespoons light brown sugar
6 packets (1 gram each) aspartame sweetener
2 tablespoons cornstarch
$\frac{1}{4}$ teaspoon freshly grated nutmeg
1 large egg, lightly beaten
$\frac{1}{2}$ cup unsweetened apple juice
$\frac{1}{2}$ cup evaporated skim milk
1 tablespoon lemon juice
1 tablespoon Poire William (pear *eau de vie*) or 1 tablespoon light rum
5 large ripe pears

For the Crust: Prepare the piecrust as recipe directs, roll thin and fit into a 9″ pie pan, making a high fluted edge. Set aside.

For the Filling: Combine the sugar, sweetener and cornstarch, pressing out all lumps. Mix in the nutmeg, egg, apple juice, milk, lemon juice and Poire William. Beat until smooth.

NOTE: If you have a food processor, you can buzz up all of these ingredients in a single 60-second churning in a work bowl fitted with the metal chopping blade.

One at a time halve the pears, peel, quarter, core, then slice thin directly into the pie shell. Pour in the liquid mixture and bake the pie uncovered in a hot oven (400°F.) for 10 minutes;

reduce the heat to moderate (350°F.) and bake 35 to 40 minutes longer or until the filling is set and touched with gold. Remove the pie from the oven and cool 30 minutes before cutting. 184 calories per serving.

RUBY-GLAZED FRESH PEACH TART
Serves 8

An unusually pretty pie and a perfect choice for a party dinner because the pie can be made well ahead of time and pulled from the refrigerator shortly before serving.

Crust:

  6 gingersnaps, buzzed to fine crumbs
  6 graham crackers (the double variety measuring 5″
      long and 2¼″ wide), buzzed to fine crumbs
  5 teaspoons melted unsalted butter

Filling:

  1 tablespoon plus 1 teaspoon cornstarch
  4 tablespoons light brown sugar, each firmly packed
  2 packets (1 gram each) aspartame sweetener
  ¼ teaspoon finely grated lemon rind
  1 large egg, lightly beaten
  1¼ cups buttermilk
  3 tablespoons heavy cream
  ¼ teaspoon ground mace
  ¾ teaspoon vanilla
  ¼ teaspoon almond extract

Topping:

  Juice of 1 large lemon
  2 packets (1 gram each) aspartame sweetener
  2 cups water
  2 very large, very ripe peaches

Glaze:

  ¾ cup cranberry juice cocktail
  1 tablespoon arrowroot

For the Crust: Toss the gingersnap and graham-cracker crumbs with the melted butter, then pat firmly over the bottom and up the sides of a 9" pie pan. Set aside while you prepare the filling.

For the Filling: Blend the cornstarch with the brown sugar and sweetener, pressing out all lumps; mix in the lemon rind and all remaining filling ingredients. Pour into the prepared crust and bake in a moderate oven (350°F.) for 15 to 20 minutes, just until filling is softly set.

Meanwhile, Prepare the Topping: In a large shallow mixing bowl, combine the lemon juice, sweetener and water (this is acidulated water into which you will drop the peaches as you slice them to prevent them from turning brown). Peel the peaches one at a time, halve, pit and slice very thin lengthwise (from stem end to blossom end). As you slice each half, keep the slices in order and stack them together, then slide gently into the acidulated water. (There's a reason for keeping the slices in order; you can fan them out easily on top of the filling and they will be perfectly matched). Keep the sliced peaches submerged in the acidulated water until you need them.

For the Glaze: In a shaker jar, combine the cranberry juice cocktail and the arrowroot by shaking vigorously. Dump into a small, heavy stainless steel saucepan, set over moderately low heat and whisk 3 to 4 minutes, just until the mixture thickens and clears. Remove from the heat at once.

To Assemble the Tart: As soon as the filling is softly set, remove the tart from the oven. Quickly pat the peach slices dry on paper toweling (I pick up the stacked slices and blot gently in paper toweling). Arrange the peach slices, slightly overlapping, around the edge of the tart, then add an inner circle of overlapping peach slices in the center. Spoon the glaze evenly over all, then chill well hours before cutting. 158 calories per serving.

OLD SOUTH BUTTERMILK PIE
Serves 8

A tart, low-calorie custard pie, thanks to the buttermilk and the substitution of heavy cream for melted butter.

Crumb Crust:

   6 graham crackers (the double variety measuring 5″
      long and $2\frac{1}{4}$″ wide), buzzed to fine crumbs
   5 vanilla wafers, buzzed to fine crumbs
   5 teaspoons melted unsalted butter

Buttermilk Filling:

   2 large eggs, lightly beaten
   $\frac{1}{2}$ cup sugar
   1 tablespoon flour
   $1\frac{1}{3}$ cups buttermilk
   $\frac{1}{3}$ cup heavy cream
   1 teaspoon vanilla
   $\frac{1}{4}$ teaspoon freshly grated nutmeg

For the Crust: Toss the graham-cracker and vanilla-wafer crumbs with the melted butter, then pat firmly over the bottom and up the sides of a 9″ pie pan. Set aside.

For the Filling: Beat the eggs with the sugar and flour until smooth; combine the buttermilk, heavy cream and vanilla, then blend into the sugar mixture. Pour into the crumb crust and sprinkle the nutmeg evenly on top. Bake in a slow oven (300°F.) for 45 minutes or until softly set.

   Remove from the oven and cool 30 minutes before cutting. Or, if you prefer, chill well before serving. 175 calories per serving.

BANANA CREAM PIE
Serves 8

Uncommonly rich and yet just 136 calories per serving.

Crust:

  1 generous spraying of nonstick vegetable cooking
      spray
  5 graham crackers (the double variety measuring 5″
      long and $2\frac{1}{4}''$ wide), buzzed to fine crumbs

Filling:

  $1\frac{1}{2}$ cups evaporated skim milk
  1 cup milk
  $\frac{1}{2}$ cup half-and-half cream
  1 envelope plus 1 teaspoon plain gelatin
  2 large egg yolks, lightly beaten
  8 packets (1 gram each) aspartame sweetener
  $1\frac{1}{2}$ teaspoons vanilla
  2 small ripe bananas
    Juice of $\frac{1}{2}$ lemon

For the Crust: Spray the bottom and sides of a 9″ pie pan with the nonstick cooking spray, dump in the cracker crumbs, then tilt the pan from one side to another until the sides are evenly coated; spread all loose crumbs as evenly as possible over the bottom of the pan. Set aside while you prepare the filling.

For the Filling: Place the evaporated skim milk, milk and half-and-half in a medium-size heavy saucepan, sprinkle the gelatin evenly over the surface, set over moderate heat and cook and stir 3 to 4 minutes until the gelatin dissolves completely. Whisk a little of the hot milk mixture into the yolks, stir back into pan and cook and stir about a minute longer; do not boil or the mixture may curdle. Remove from the heat and cool to almost room temperature; whisk the mixture often to prevent a skin from forming on the surface. Beat in the sweetener and vanilla, then chill the filling several hours in the refrigerator (or about 45 minutes in the freezer) until it mounds softly. Whisk hard until creamy.

Now peel one of the bananas and slice thin, slightly on the diagonal, and arrange evenly over the bottom of the pie crust. Pour in the filling. Peel and slice the remaining banana the same way; dip the slices into lemon juice (this is to keep them from darkening) and arrange in a sunburst pattern over the top of the pie.

Cover loosely with plastic food wrap and chill at least 12 hours. To serve, cut into 8 wedges. 136 calories per serving.

CHOCOLATE SATIN PIE
Serves 8

Dense, dark and deceptively rich.

NOTE: For proper flavor and texture, use silken nagari tofu because it is naturally sweet and can be beaten to satiny smoothness. You'll find it in health food stores, Oriental groceries, even in some supermarkets.

Crust:

> 1 generous spraying of nonstick vegetable cooking spray
> 4 old-fashioned thin chocolate wafers (those that are 2¼" in diameter), buzzed to fine crumbs

Filling:

> ⅔ cup sugar
> 5 tablespoons Dutch-process cocoa powder (not a mix)
> ½ cup evaporated skim milk
> 3 large eggs
> 6 ounces fresh silken nagari tofu (soybean curd)
> ½ cup sour cream
> 2 tablespoons heavy cream
> 1½ teaspoons vanilla

For the Crust: Following label directions, spray the bottom and sides of a 9" pie pan with nonstick vegetable cooking spray. Dump in the crumbs, then tilt pan from one side to the other until bottom and sides are evenly coated with crumbs; tap out excess crumbs. Set pan aside.

For the Filling: Combine the sugar and cocoa, pressing out all lumps. Now combine cocoa mixture with all remaining filling ingredients in a food processor fitted with the metal chopping blade, in an electric blender or in a mixer set at high speed. Blend several minutes until creamy smooth (no lumps of tofu

28

should be discernible). Pour the filling into prepared pan and bake uncovered in a moderately slow oven (325°F.) for 40 minutes or until set like custard. Remove pie from oven, set on a wire rack and cool to room temperature.

NOTE: The filling will pull from the sides of the pan, but that is as it should be.

Cover pie and chill several hours. Cut into 8 wedges and serve. 188 calories per serving.

OLD-TIMEY LEMON MERINGUE PIE
Serves 8

Very tart, very good.

Crust:

    1 recipe Pared-Down Piecrust (see p. 51)

Filling:

    1½ cups water
    ½ cup cornstarch
      Rind of 1 large lemon, grated fine
      Juice of 2 large lemons
    3 egg yolks, lightly beaten
    1 teaspoon unsalted butter
   15 packets (1 gram each) aspartame sweetener

Meringue:

    3 large egg whites
      Pinch salt
    4 tablespoons granulated sugar
    1 tablespoon confectioners' (10X) sugar
    1 teaspoon lemon juice

For the Crust: Prepare and roll Pared-Down Piecrust, fit into a 9″ pie pan and bake as the recipe directs; cool to room temperature.

For the Filling: In a shaker jar (or in a food processor fitted with the metal chopping blade), combine the water and cornstarch until absolutely homogeneous. Pour into a small heavy saucepan (not aluminum, which may give the filling a metallic taste), add the lemon rind and juice, set over moderately low heat and whisk about 3 minutes until mixture thickens and clears (it will be very thick). Whisk a little of the hot cornstarch mixture into

30

the egg yolks, stir back into the pan and stir about 1 minute—just until no raw egg flavor remains. Remove from the heat, whisk in the butter, then cool to lukewarm, whisking often. Mix in the sweetener and pour into the baked pie shell.

For the Meringue: Beat the egg whites with the salt until frothy, then begin adding the granulated sugar a tablespoon at a time, beating all the while until soft peaks form when you withdraw the beater. Add the 10X sugar and lemon juice and continue beating to stiff peaks.

Spread the meringue on top of the lemon filling, swirling it into peaks and valleys and making sure that it touches the crust all around (if the meringue does not touch the crust at all points, it will shrink, forming an island of meringue on top of the filling).

Bake in a hot oven (400°F.) for about 5 minutes or until the meringue is lightly browned. Cool the pie 30 minutes, then cut into 8 wedges and serve. 182 calories per serving.

FRESH LIME ANGEL PIE
Serves 8

A heavenly lime dessert!

NOTE: You must use freshly squeezed lime juice for this recipe; otherwise the pie will not have the proper flavor.

Crust:

1 recipe Angel Pie Shell (see p. 53)

Filling:

½ cup water
1 envelope plain gelatin
3 large eggs, separated
½ cup evaporated skim milk
½ cup freshly squeezed lime juice (you'll need about 3 limes)
Finely grated rind of 1 lime
12 packets (1 gram each) aspartame sweetener
3 tablespoons heavy cream
Pinch cream of tartar
Pinch salt

For the Crust: Prepare the Angel Pie Shell as directed and set aside.

For the Filling: Place the water in a small heavy saucepan, sprinkle the gelatin evenly over the surface and let stand a few minutes. Set over moderate heat and stir 3 to 4 minutes until the gelatin dissolves completely. Beat the egg yolks with the milk, whisk in a little of the hot gelatin mixture, stir back into pan, set over low heat and cook and stir 2 to 3 minutes until slightly thickened (do not allow to boil or the mixture may curdle). Remove from the heat, pour into a medium-size mixing bowl and cool to room temperature; stir now and then to prevent a skin from forming on the surface of the sauce.

Add the lime juice in a thin stream, whisking hard, then mix in the lime rind, sweetener and heavy cream. Cover and chill until thick and syrupy—about 1 hour.

Beat the gelatin mixture at highest mixer speed until frothy. Also beat the egg whites with the cream of tartar and salt to stiff peaks. Fold the egg whites gently but thoroughly into the whipped gelatin mixture.

NOTE: Resist the impulse to tint the filling green; its natural color—pale, pale Key-lime green—is much prettier to my taste.

Spoon the filling into the Angel Pie Shell and chill at least 8 hours before cutting and serving. 110 calories per serving.

Variations:

Lemon Angel Pie: Prepare exactly as directed, but substitute fresh lemon juice and rind for the lime juice and rind. 110 calories per serving.

Orange Angel Pie: Place $\frac{1}{2}$ cup freshly squeezed orange juice in a small heavy saucepan, sprinkle the gelatin evenly over the surface, then heat and dissolve as directed. From this point on, prepare exactly as directed for the Lime Angel Pie, but substitute $\frac{1}{2}$ cup freshly squeezed orange juice and 1 tablespoon finely grated orange rind for the lime juice and rind and use 6 packets of aspartame sweetener instead of 12. 114 calories per serving.

PUMPKIN CHIFFON PIE IN GINGERSNAP CRUST

Serves 8

Incredibly creamy and rich and yet less than 150 calories (!) per serving.

Gingersnap Crust:

1 generous spraying of nonstick vegetable cooking spray
5 gingersnaps (those measuring 2″ in diameter), buzzed to fine crumbs
3 graham crackers (the double variety measuring 5″ long and $2\frac{1}{4}$″ wide), buzzed to fine crumbs
4 teaspoons melted unsalted butter

Pumpkin Chiffon Filling:

1 cup evaporated milk
1 envelope plain gelatin
$\frac{1}{2}$ teaspoon ground cinnamon
$\frac{1}{4}$ teaspoon ground nutmeg
$\frac{1}{4}$ teaspoon ground ginger
Pinch ground cloves
2 eggs, separated
1 can (1 pound) unsweetened solid-pack pumpkin
Rind of 1 orange, grated fine
5 packets (1 gram each) aspartame sweetener
Pinch salt
3 tablespoons superfine sugar

For the Crust: Spray the bottom and sides of a 9″ pie pan with the nonstick vegetable spray. Toss the gingersnap and graham-cracker crumbs with the melted butter, then pat firmly over the bottom and up the sides of the pie pan. Set aside.

For the Filling: Place the milk in a small heavy saucepan; sprinkle in the gelatin, cinnamon, nutmeg, ginger and cloves and let

34

stand 5 minutes. Set over moderate heat and stir 3 to 4 minutes until gelatin is completely dissolved. Beat the egg yolks until frothy, whisk in a little of the hot milk mixture, stir back into pan and cook and stir about 1 minute—just long enough to cook the egg yolks. Under no circumstances allow the mixture to boil or it may curdle.

Remove the mixture from the heat and combine with the pumpkin and orange rind in a large heatproof bowl. Cool to room temperature, then mix in the sweetener.

Sprinkle the salt over the egg whites and beat until frothy. Add 1 tablespoon of the sugar and beat until silvery; add another tablespoon of sugar and beat to soft peaks; add the final tablespoon of sugar and beat *almost,* but not quite, to stiff peaks—the peaks will lop over at the very top when the beater is withdrawn.

Fold the beaten whites into the pumpkin mixture until no streaks of white or orange remain. Pour into pie shell, swirling the surface into hills and valleys. Chill at least 6 hours before cutting. Trim, if you like, with orange twists or slices and mint sprigs. 147 calories per serving.

SKY-HIGH LEMON CHIFFON PIE
Serves 8

Cool and creamy and would you believe just 122 calories per serving?

Crust:

>   6 graham crackers (the double variety measuring 5″
>   long and $2\frac{1}{4}$″ wide), buzzed to fine crumbs
>   1 tablespoon plus 2 teaspoons melted unsalted butter

Filling:

> $\frac{1}{2}$ cup water
>   Juice of $2\frac{1}{2}$ large lemons
>   1 envelope plain gelatin
>   4 large eggs, separated
>   Rind of 1 large lemon, grated fine
> 20 packets (1 gram each) aspartame sweetener
>   Pinch salt
>   4 tablespoons superfine sugar

For the Crust: Toss the crumbs well with the melted butter, then pat firmly over the bottom and up the sides of a 9″ pie pan; set aside while you prepare the filling.

For the Filling: Place the water and lemon juice in a small heavy saucepan (not aluminum, which might make the filling taste of metal); sprinkle the gelatin evenly over the surface and let stand 1 minute. Add the egg yolks and whisk well to combine. Set over moderately low heat and stir constantly for about 5 minutes, just until all gelatin is dissolved and the sauce is the consistency of a thin custard sauce (do not boil or the sauce may curdle). Remove from the heat, stir in the lemon rind and cool quickly by setting in an ice bath; whisk frequently. As soon as the filling has cooled, whisk in the sweetener. Continue to whisk in the ice-water bath until the gelatin begins to thicken—it should be quite syrupy.

Beat the egg whites with the salt until frothy; add 1 tablespoon of the sugar and beat until silvery; now continue beating the whites, adding the remaining sugar, 1 tablespoon at a time, until they stand in stiff peaks when the beater is withdrawn. Fold the whites gently but thoroughly into the lemon mixture, spoon into the prepared crust, swirling the filling into hills and valleys.

Chill 3 to 4 hours until firm, then cut into 8 wedges and serve. 122 calories per serving.

GRAND MARNIER CHIFFON PIE
Serves 8

Elegant enough for a party, yet uncommonly easy to make. Decorate, if you like, with poufs of Low-Calorie Whipped "Cream" (see p. 178), shreds of orange zest and tiny sprigs of lemon verbena or mint.

Crust:

> 6 graham crackers (the double variety measuring 5″
>   long and 2¼″ wide), buzzed to fine crumbs
> 1 tablespoon plus 2 teaspoons melted unsalted butter

Filling:

> 1 cup freshly squeezed orange juice
> 1 tablespoon lemon juice
> 1 envelope plain gelatin
> 4 large eggs, separated
>   Rind of 1 orange, grated very fine
> 10 packets (1 gram each) aspartame sweetener
> 2 tablespoons Grand Marnier
>   Pinch salt
> 4 tablespoons superfine sugar

For the Crust: Toss the crumbs well with the melted butter, then pat firmly over the bottom and up the sides of a 9″ pie pan; set aside while you prepare the filling.

For the Filling: Place the orange and lemon juice in a small saucepan, preferably stainless steel, flameproof glass or enameled cast iron so that the sauce doesn't take on a metallic taste; sprinkle the gelatin evenly over the surface and set aside. Whisk in the egg yolks, set over moderately low heat and stir constantly for about 5 minutes, just until all gelatin is dissolved and the sauce is the consistency of a thin custard sauce (do not allow the sauce to boil or it may curdle). Remove from the heat, stir in the orange rind, and set in an ice bath and whisk often until the mixture cools to room temperature; stir in the sweetener and Grand Marnier, then continue whisking over the ice-water bath until the mixture is very thick and syrupy.

Beat the egg whites with the salt until frothy; add 1 tablespoon of the sugar and beat until silvery; now continue beating the whites, adding the remaining sugar 1 tablespoon at a time, until thcy stand in stiff pcaks when you withdraw the beater. Gently but thoroughly fold the whites into the Grand Marnier mixture, spoon into the prepared crust, swirling the filling into hills and valleys.

Chill the pie 3 to 4 hours or until firm, then cut into 8 wedges and serve. 141 calories per serving.

LIGHT AND LOVELY LEMON CHEESECAKE

Serves 12

If the cheesecake is to be creamy smooth, the ricotta cheese, yogurt and egg yolk used in the filling must be at room temperature. Serve the cheesecake as is, or top with Pineapple-Ginger, Cherry or Cran-Apple Cheesecake Topping (see pp. 181, 182 and 183).

Crust:

> 8 pieces zwieback toast, buzzed to fine crumbs
> 1 tablespoon melted butter or margarine
> ⅛ teaspoon ground cinnamon

Filling:

> 2 tablespoons orange juice
> 2 tablespoons plus 1 teaspoon lemon juice
> 2 envelopes plain gelatin
> 1 pound ricotta cheese, at room temperature
> 1 carton (8 ounces) lowfat lemon-flavored yogurt, at
>   room temperature
> ½ cup sugar
> 1 egg yolk, at room temperature
> 1 teaspoon finely grated lemon rind
> ½ teaspoon vanilla
> ½ cup ice-cold evaporated milk

For the Crust: Toss the crumbs with the melted butter and cinnamon and press evenly over the bottom of an 8″ springform pan. Set in the freezer or refrigerator to chill while you prepare the filling.

For the Filling: Place the orange juice and 2 tablespoons of the lemon juice in a very small saucepan; sprinkle in the gelatin and let stand several minutes until softened. Set over moderate heat and stir 3 to 4 minutes until gelatin dissolves. Remove from the heat and cool.

In a food processor fitted with the metal chopping blade or in an electric mixer set at high speed, blend the ricotta cheese, yogurt, sugar, egg yolk, lemon rind and vanilla until uniformly smooth; beat in the cooled gelatin mixture and set aside.

Whip the ice-cold evaporated milk and the 1 teaspoon lemon juice to stiff peaks and fold into the cheese mixture. Pour into the springform pan and chill at least 4 hours before serving. Cut into 12 wedges and serve. 168 calories per serving.

MOCHA CHEESECAKE

Serves 12

It's important that the cheeses and egg yolk used in this recipe be at room temperature, not refrigerator-cold, because the gelatin will gel too quickly and the cheesecake will not be smooth. The whipped cream garnish is entirely optional (but highly desirable) and adds a mere 23 calories to each portion.

Crust:

> 10 old-fashioned thin chocolate wafers (those measuring $2\frac{1}{4}''$ in diameter), buzzed to fine crumbs
> 1 tablespoon melted butter or margarine

Filling:

> $\frac{1}{3}$ cup water
> 1 envelope plus 1 teaspoon plain gelatin
> 2 teaspoons instant-espresso powder
> 1 pound ricotta cheese, at room temperature
> 1 package (3 ounces) cream cheese, at room temperature
> $\frac{3}{4}$ cup sifted cocoa powder (not a mix)
> $\frac{1}{2}$ cup plus 2 tablespoons sugar
> 1 egg yolk, at room temperature
> $\frac{1}{2}$ cup ice-cold evaporated milk
> 1 teaspoon lemon juice
> 1 teaspoon vanilla

Garnish (Optional):

> $\frac{1}{3}$ cup heavy cream, whipped

For the Crust: Toss the crumbs with the melted butter and press evenly over the bottom of an 8″ springform pan. Set the pan in either the freezer or refrigerator to chill while you prepare the filling.

For the Filling: Pour the water into a small heavy saucepan and sprinkle in the gelatin. Let stand a few minutes to soften the gelatin, then set over moderate heat and stir 3 to 4 minutes until gelatin dissolves completely. Stir in the espresso powder, remove from the heat and set aside to cool.

In a food processor fitted with the metal chopping blade or in an electric mixer set at high speed, combine the ricotta, cream cheese, cocoa, $\frac{1}{2}$ cup sugar and egg yolk. Beat hard until silky smooth, then beat in the cooled gelatin mixture and set aside.

Whip the ice-cold evaporated milk and lemon juice to stiff peaks; beat in the remaining 2 tablespoons of sugar and the vanilla. Fold into the cheese mixture, pour into the springform pan and chill at least 4 hours before serving. Cut into 12 wedges and serve.

For the Garnish: Fit a pastry tube with a star tip and fill with the whipped cream. Pipe 12 rosettes around the top edge of the cheesecake (this gives everyone a taste of cream). If there's any whipped cream remaining, pipe a design in the center of the cheesecake. 207 calories per serving *without* the whipped cream garnish; 230 calories per serving *with*.

CRÊPES SUZETTE
Serves 4

These are not flamed at table as they are in pricey restaurants, yet I think you'll find these slimmed-down crêpes almost as good as the more caloric French original.

Crêpes:

  1 recipe Basic Crêpe Batter (see p. 59)
  Rind of 1 orange, grated very fine

Filling:

  Rind of 2 oranges, cut into fine julienne
  Juice of 6 oranges
  1 teaspoon unsalted butter, at room temperature
  1 tablespoon Grand Marnier

Topping:

  $\frac{1}{2}$ cup plain yogurt
  $1\frac{1}{2}$ packets (1 gram each) aspartame sweetener
  $\frac{1}{2}$ teaspoon Grand Marnier

For the Crêpes: Prepare the batter according to the recipe, adding to it the grated orange rind. Cook the crêpes as directed (you will need only 8 of them, so the extra one can be the cook's reward provided he/she isn't dieting). Set the crêpes aside.

For the Filling: Blanch the orange rind in rapidly boiling water for 2 minutes, plunge into cold water, then drain and set aside. Place the orange juice in a medium-size heavy saucepan (not aluminum, which may make the filling taste of metal), set uncovered over moderately high heat and boil until reduced to about $\frac{1}{2}$ cup—this should take 7 to 8 minutes; add the julienned rind for the last 2 to 3 minutes of reduction. Off the heat, blend in the butter and Grand Marnier.

To Assemble the Crêpes: Spread 1 tablespoon of the orange mixture on each crêpe, fold the crêpe in half, then in half again, forming quarters. Put the crêpes in a single layer in a shallow baking pan or au gratin pan that has been lightly sprayed with nonstick vegetable cooking spray, and heat, uncovered, in a moderate oven (350°F.) for 5 minutes.

Meanwhile, Combine All Topping Ingredients: Serve the crêpes at once, topped by the yogurt sauce. 232 calories per serving.

STRAWBERRY CHEESE BLINTZES
Serves 4

Really very good, the perfect dessert for a light summer luncheon.

Blintzes:

    1 recipe Basic Crêpe Batter (see p. 59)
    Rind of 1 lemon, grated very fine

Filling:

    1 cup lowfat cottage cheese
    $\frac{1}{2}$ cup plain yogurt
    1 packet (1 gram) aspartame sweetener
    2 large egg yolks
    $\frac{1}{2}$ teaspoon ground cinnamon
    $\frac{1}{2}$ teaspoon almond extract
    $\frac{1}{2}$ teaspoon vanilla

Topping:

    1 cup very thinly sliced fresh strawberries (sweeten, if
        needed, with a little aspartame sweetener)

For the Blintzes: Prepare the batter according to the recipe, adding to it the grated lemon rind. Cook the crêpes as directed (you'll need 8 only for this recipe, so consider the extra one a bonus). Set the crêpes aside.

For the Filling: Buzz all ingredients until creamy smooth in a food processor fitted with the metal chopping blade, in an electric blender at high speed or by beating at highest mixer speed.

To Assemble Blintzes: Place 3 tablespoons of the cheese mixture in the center of each crêpe, fold the right and left sides in, over the filling, then the tops and bottoms, forming "envelopes."

NOTE: You'll have to work fast since the filling is very soft. Place the blintzes seam-side down in a shallow baking pan that you have sprayed lightly with nonstick vegetable cooking spray.

Bake the blintzes uncovered in a moderate oven (350°F.) for 20 to 25 minutes or until firm. Serve at once topped by the strawberries. 210 calories per serving.

CREAM PUFFS
Makes 12

Mouthwatering pastries that are everyone's favorite. It's important that you choose a dry sunny day for making cream puffs; otherwise they will wilt almost as soon as you pull them from the oven.

> 1 recipe Pâte à Choux (see p. 56)
> 1 recipe Crème Patissière, well chilled (see p. 160)
> 2 tablespoons milk (glaze)
> 2 tablespoons vanilla sugar*

For the Puffs: Prepare the Pâte à Choux as directed, then drop from rounded tablespoonfuls onto ungreased baking sheets, spacing the puffs 3″ apart (you can only get 6 puffs on each baking sheet). Dip a pastry brush into the milk and brush the top of each puff lightly. Bake in a hot oven (400°F.) 35 to 40 minutes (don't peek for the first 20 minutes), until the puffs are a rich nut brown and sound hollow when you thump them with your fingers. Remove the cream puffs from the oven and transfer to wire racks to cool.

To Assemble the Puffs: Slice 1″ off the top of each cream puff, reach down inside and pull out and discard all soft, doughy bits. Now spoon the chilled Crème Patissière into the hollow of each puff (about 2½ tablespoons per puff), replace the tops and sift the vanilla sugar lightly over the tops. Serve at once.

NOTE: The cream filling spoils fairly fast, so if you cannot serve the cream puffs straight away, refrigerate them—but be forewarned, the puffs will lose their crispness. 120 calories per Cream Puff.

---

*You can buy vanilla sugar in specialty food shops or you can make it yourself by filling a cannister with confectioners' sugar, pushing 2 vanilla beans deep down into the sugar and letting it season for at least a week. Keep the vanilla beans in the sugar and when you have used it all up, simply refill the cannister with sugar and reseason. 23 calories per tablespoon.

CHOCOLATE ÉCLAIRS
Makes 12

Only 150 calories per pastry! Make on a bright, sunny day, not in humid or rainy weather, because the éclairs will go soggy.

> 1 recipe Pâte à Choux (see p. 56)
> 1 recipe Crème Patissière, well chilled (see p. 160)
> 2 tablespoons milk (glaze)

Chocolate Icing:

> $\frac{3}{4}$ cup unsifted confectioners' (10X) sugar
> 3 tablespoons cocoa powder (not a mix)
> $4\frac{1}{2}$ teaspoons very hot water
> $1\frac{1}{2}$ teaspoons unsalted butter, at room temperature
> $\frac{3}{4}$ teaspoon vanilla

For the Éclairs: Prepare the Pâte à Choux as directed, spoon into a pastry bag fitted with a large plain tip, then pipe onto ungreased baking sheets in strips about $3\frac{1}{2}''$ x $1\frac{1}{2}''$ x $1''$, spacing them well apart. Dip a pastry brush into the milk and lightly brush the top of each pastry. Bake in a hot oven (400°F.) for 35 to 40 minutes (no peeking during the first half of baking) until nicely browned and the pastries sound hollow when you thump them with your fingers. Remove the pastries from the oven, transfer at once to wire racks and cool to room temperature.

Halve each pastry lengthwise, pull out and discard all soft spongy portions inside; now fill the pastry bottoms with Crème Patissière (allow about $2\frac{1}{2}$ tablespoons per éclair), replace the tops and set aside for the time being.

For the Chocolate Icing: Stir together the 10X sugar and cocoa, pressing out any lumps. Add the water and stir until smooth; blend in the butter and vanilla.

Frost the top of each éclair, then allow the icing to harden for 20 to 30 minutes. Serve the éclairs at once and if you must keep them for a while, store them in the refrigerator even though they will lose their lovely crispness (unless kept well chilled, the pastry cream filling may spoil). 150 calories per Éclair.

Variations:

Double Chocolate Éclairs: Prepare the éclairs as directed, but fill with Crème Patissière au Chocolat (see page 160) instead of the more conventional pastry cream. 158 calories per Éclair.

Chocolate-Orange Éclairs: Prepare the éclairs as directed, but fill with Crème Patissière à l'Orange (see page 161). 150 calories per Éclair.

PARED-DOWN PIECRUST
Makes a 9" Pie Shell

This piecrust is pared down in calories—by some 60 calories per serving. Yet despite its reduced shortening content, it is surprisingly flaky provided you do not overwork it.

- $\frac{3}{4}$ cup sifted all-purpose flour
- 2 tablespoons cornstarch
- $\frac{1}{4}$ teaspoon salt
- 3 tablespoons vegetable shortening, at room temperature
- 4 tablespoons ice-cold water (about)

In a shallow mixing bowl, combine the flour, cornstarch and salt. Using a pastry blender, cut the shortening into the dry ingredients until the texture of coarse meal. Now forking the mixture briskly, scatter the ice water, 1 tablespoon at a time, over the surface of the dry ingredients. The instant the dry ingredients are moistened and adhere together, stop mixing. Shape the mixture lightly into a ball, place on a very lightly floured pastry cloth (I use as little as 1 tablespoon of flour and spread it in a circle in the center of the cloth). Now flatten the pastry gently with a very lightly floured, stockinette-covered rolling pin.

NOTE: By using a pastry cloth, and a stockinette, you can use a minimal amount of flour with little risk of the pastry's sticking.

With short, quick, light strokes, work from the center of the pastry outward, rolling into a thin circle about $2\frac{1}{2}''$ larger in diameter than the pie pan you intend to use. Even up any ragged edges as you roll, also patch any broken or thin spots by cutting off ragged trimmings and "glueing" them into place with a little cold water.

Once the pastry circle is rolled to the proper size, lay the rolling pin straight across the center; very gently lop half of the pastry over the rolling pin, ease it into the pan and fit it against the bottom and sides. Trim the overhang so that it is about $\frac{3}{4}''$ larger all around than the pan, then roll it under, and on top of, the rim; crimp with your fingers making a decorative fluted edge. The pie shell is now ready to fill.

To Bake the Pie Shell Before It's Filled: Many recipes call for baked pie shells and this one can be "blind baked" as successfully as those made of richer pastries. First, prick the bottom and sides of the pie shell well with a fork to allow steam a means of escape (this will minimize buckling). Second, line the pie shell with wax paper or baking parchment, fill with pie weights, dried beans or raw rice (to reduce shrinkage). Bake in a hot oven (425°F.) for 10 to 12 minutes, just until the color of old ivory. Remove from the oven, lift out the paper of weights and cool the pie shell to room temperature before filling.

To Seal the Piecrust: Certain juicy or liquid fillings will seep into pastry and make it soggy unless it is first sealed. All you need do is beat an egg white with a tablespoon of cold water until frothy, then brush it generously over the sides and bottom of the pie shell; allow to air-dry about 20 minutes before filling. 674 calories total; 84 for each of 8 servings.

ANGEL PIE SHELL
Makes a 9" Pie Shell

An angel crust is nothing more than a meringue spooned into a pie pan and sculpted into a shallow shell. It's beautiful, it's versatile, and best of all, it contains a mere 41 calories for each of 8 servings as compared to 150 calories for standard pastry. The angel shell, moreover, is the perfect repository for all manner of gelatin mousses and chiffons (lime, lemon, orange, pumpkin, chocolate, etc.) for custard fillings (vanilla, butterscotch, chocolate), even for sherbets and fresh fruits.

NOTE: It's imperative that you choose a dry, sunny day for making the Angel Pie Shell; in humid weather, it will absorb atmospheric moisture and lose its exquisite crispness.

  3 large egg whites
    Pinch cream of tartar
    Pinch salt
  6 tablespoons superfine sugar

Place the egg whites, cream of tartar and salt in the largest mixer bowl and beat until frothy. Add 1 tablespoon of the sugar and beat until silvery, add another tablespoon and beat until frothy. Now, with the mixer running at moderate speed, continue adding the sugar gradually, a tablespoon at a time. After all of the sugar has been incorporated, beat several minutes at highest mixer speed until the meringue is very stiff and dry (if you cut through it with a knife, the edges of the cut should remain crisp and sharp).

Using a rubber spatula, spoon the meringue into an ungreased 9" pie pan and smooth it over the bottom and up the sides, making a high, rounded edge. Take care not to let the meringue overhang the rim or it may shatter when you cut the pie.

Bake in a very slow oven (275°F.) for 1 hour and 15 minutes, then turn the oven off and let the pie shell stand in the oven until the oven is completely cold. 41 calories for each of 8 wedges.

MERINGUE LAYERS
Makes Three 9" Round Layers

These cloud-light layers can be used as the foundation of Dacquoise (see p. 187) and a variety of vacherins (nests or stackcakes made of meringue and fresh fruits or fruit sherbets). They can also be sandwiched together with cool, feathery mousses.

NOTE: Don't attempt to make these meringues in less than perfect weather; they will absorb atmospheric moisture and on a truly humid day will go as limp as a Dali watch.

> 6 large egg whites
> Pinch salt
> Pinch cream of tartar
> ¾ cup superfine sugar
> 3 light sprayings of nonstick vegetable cooking spray

Whip the egg whites with the salt and cream of tartar until frothy; add 1 tablespoon of the sugar and beat until silvery. Add another tablespoon of sugar and beat just until mixture begins to thicken. Continue beating at moderate mixer speed, adding the sugar gradually, 1 tablespoon at a time. After all of the sugar has been incorporated, turn the mixer to its highest speed and beat the meringue hard for 5 minutes nonstop. The mixture should be so stiff that when you cut through it with a knife, the edges of the cut remain crisp and sharp.

Turn three 9" layer-cake pans upside down and spray the bottom of each lightly with nonstick vegetable cooking spray. Divide the meringue into three equal parts and spread thickly on the bottoms of the cake pans, smoothing the tops of two meringues as evenly as possible and swirling the third into hills and valleys (this will be the top layer).

NOTE: The best implements to use for spreading the meringue are a rubber spatula and a long, thin-blade spatula. Make certain that the edges of the meringue are flush with the edge of the pan; if it overhangs the pan at any point, the meringue will be difficult to remove from the pan bottom.

Bake the meringue on the middle rack of a very slow oven (275°F.) for 1 hour and 15 minutes.

NOTE: If your oven is not large enough to accommodate all three layers on a single rack, place one rack slightly above the center and one slightly below the center; bake two layers on the upper rack and the third layer on the lower rack. As soon as the meringues have baked the allotted time, turn the oven off and let the meringues stay in the oven until it is stone-cold.

Remove the meringues from the oven; loosen each layer gently around the edge with a small, thin-blade spatula. The meringue should pop right off the pan bottom; if it doesn't, twist the meringue slightly. If it still doesn't dislodge, loosen all the way around the edge with the spatula.

Sandwich the meringues together with sherbet, with a favorite light mousse, or use in making Dacquoise or Vacherin aux Framboises (see pp. 187 and 189). 654 calories for all three layers; 218 calories per layer.

NOTE: Because of their richness, vacherins and dacquoises are usually cut into 12 wedges, which brings the calorie count down out of the stratosphere.

PÂTE À CHOUX (CHOUX PASTRY)
Makes 12 Cream Puffs or Éclairs

Cream puffs and éclairs are scarcely something we think of as low calorie, and yet by way of a little kitchen alchemy, I've managed to slash the calories of choux pastry by almost 50 percent. And I've cut the calories of the traditional cream puff and éclair filling (Crème Patissière; see p. 160) even more. Put the two together and cream puffs and éclairs do indeed qualify as unforbidden sweets.

        1 cup water
        5 tablespoons unsalted butter
        $\frac{1}{4}$ teaspoon salt
        $\frac{1}{2}$ cup sifted all-purpose flour
        $\frac{1}{4}$ cup sifted cornstarch
        3 large eggs, at room temperature

Place the water, butter and salt in a small heavy saucepan and set aside for the moment. Sift the flour with the cornstarch twice onto a piece of wax paper. Set the saucepan over moderate heat and bring the butter mixture to a full rolling boil; remove from the heat and dump in the cornstarch mixture, whisking hard all the while. Keep whisking until the mixture comes together in a ball. Now break one of the eggs into the saucepan and whisk vigorously until it is completely incorporated in the pastry. Add another egg, beat until the mixture is completely smooth, then break in the final egg. Again beat until the pastry is absolutely smooth. The pastry is now ready to use in making Cream Puffs and Éclairs (see pp. 48 and 49). 70 calories for each of 12 Cream Puffs or Éclairs (unfilled and unfrosted).

DROP SHORTCAKES
Serves 8

By substituting heavy cream for calorie-laden shortening, by using cornstarch in place of some of the flour (it has greater thickening power than flour and yet contains virtually none of the tenacious, elastic protein of wheat flour that tends to toughen breads and pastries), and by "greasing" the pan with nonstick vegetable cooking spray instead of shortening, I've subtracted approximately 50 calories per serving from a pet shortcake recipe. And that's about what's contained in $\frac{3}{4}$ cup of sliced strawberries or peaches (sweetened to taste). Use these shortcakes as the foundation of any favorite fruit shortcake, but *do* resist the temptation to butter them hot—1 tablespoon of butter will up the calorie content by 102.

  $1\frac{1}{2}$ cups unsifted self-rising cake flour
  2 tablespoons cornstarch
  5 packets (1 gram each) aspartame sweetener
  $\frac{1}{2}$ cup heavy cream
  $\frac{1}{3}$ cup evaporated milk

In a large mixing bowl, combine the flour, cornstarch and sweetener; make a well in the center. Combine the cream and evaporated milk, dump all at once into the well, then mix briskly with a fork just until the dry ingredients are moistened and the dough holds together. Do not mix another instant at this point or the shortcakes will toughen.

Using a tablespoon, drop 8 mounds of dough of equal size onto a baking sheet that has been lightly sprayed with nonstick vegetable cooking spray. Bake in a hot oven (400°F.) for 10 to 12 minutes until lightly browned. Split the shortcakes while hot and top with fresh sliced fruit sweetened to taste with aspartame sweetener (for most berries and peaches, you will need a 1-gram packet for each $\frac{3}{4}$ cup of prepared fruit). 149 calories per Shortcake.

NOTE: For each $\frac{3}{4}$ cup of sliced ripe strawberries (sweetened with 1 packet sweetener), add 42 calories; for each $\frac{3}{4}$ cup sweetened sliced ripe peaches, add 54 calories; for each $\frac{3}{4}$ cup sweetened blackberries, add 67 calories, and for each $\frac{3}{4}$ cup sweetened ripe blueberries, add 72 calories.

BASIC CRÊPE BATTER
Makes about 9 Crêpes

Crêpes are wonderfully theatrical, and yet they're not at all difficult to make. Use this low-calorie batter for Crêpes Suzette (see p. 44) or Strawberry Cheese Blintzes (see p. 46). Or simply roll around sliced peaches, apricots or strawberries and top with another spoonful or two of fruit.

6 tablespoons all-purpose flour
2 tablespoons cornstarch
2 eggs, lightly beaten
6 tablespoons evaporated skim milk
$\frac{1}{4}$ cup water
1 generous spraying of nonstick vegetable cooking spray

Sift the flour and cornstarch into a small mixing bowl; combine the eggs, milk and water in a measuring cup. Drizzle the combined liquids into the dry ingredients, beating hard all the while.

NOTE: If you have a food processor, fit it with the metal chopping blade, add all ingredients to the work bowl in the order listed, then beat until the consistency of heavy cream using about three 5-second churnings of the motor. Chill the batter for 1 hour before you cook the crêpes.

Spray generously the bottom and sides of a 6″ skillet with the cooking spray, then warm over moderate heat for 20 to 30 seconds. Stir the crêpe batter briefly, spoon 2 tablespoonfuls of it into the skillet, then tilt the skillet from one side to the other until the batter coats the bottom of the pan thinly but evenly. Brown the crêpe 30 seconds on one side, turn with a pancake turner and brown lightly on the second side. Turn the crêpe out onto a paper-towel-lined baking sheet (be sure to put the most attractive side of the crêpe down so that it will be on the outside when you fill and roll it). Cook the remaining crêpes the same way, then fill and roll any way you fancy. 50 calories per Crêpe.

2
MOUSSES, PUDDINGS AND SOUFFLÉS

TART LEMON MOUSSE
Serves 8

"Wow! This is scrumptious," said a reed-slim young friend of mine when I gave her a bowl of this gossamer mousse to sample. "Is it *really* low in calories?" Yes, Cindi, it really *is* low in calories.

NOTE: The critical step in making any gelatin mousse is having the gelatin mixture the proper consistency before you begin folding in the beaten whites and whipped cream. It's easiest to control the chilling process if you work with the mousse mixture in an ice bath. You must whisk it often— and vigorously—lest it lump. Ideally, the mousse mixture should be about as viscous as a very fresh, unbeaten egg white. That is, it should mound slightly on a spoon, not flatten out. If you do not let the mousse mixture thicken sufficiently, it will sink to the bottom of the finished mousse, forming an unattractive layer. On the other hand, if you let it thicken too much, you will not be able to incorporate the beaten whites or whipped cream smoothly.

$\frac{1}{2}$ cup water
 Juice of 3 large lemons (about $\frac{3}{4}$ cup)
 1 envelope plain gelatin
 4 large eggs, separated
 Rind of $1\frac{1}{2}$ lemons, grated fine
 24 packets (1 gram each) aspartame sweetener
 $\frac{1}{8}$ teaspoon salt
 4 tablespoons superfine sugar
 $\frac{1}{2}$ cup heavy cream, whipped to stiff peaks

Place the water and lemon juice in a small, heavy saucepan (not aluminum, which may give the filling a metallic taste), sprinkle the gelatin evenly over the surface and let stand 5 minutes. Whisk in the egg yolks, set over moderately low heat and cook, whisking constantly, for 3 to 4 minutes until the gelatin has completely dissolved and the mixture is about the consistency of stirred custard. Do not allow to boil or the sauce may curdle. Pour into a large heatproof bowl, set in an ice bath and whisk in the lemon rind. Continue whisking the mixture until it has cooled to room temperature, then blend in the sweetener. Continue whisking the mousse mixture in the ice bath until it is quite thick and syrupy—it should mound lightly when you take up a bit of it on a spoon.

Beat the egg whites with the salt until frothy, add 1 tablespoon of the sugar and beat until silvery. Continue beating the egg whites, adding the remaining sugar, a tablespoon at a time, until they peak stiffly. Blend about $\frac{1}{2}$ cup of the whites into the mousse mixture to lighten it, then dump the remaining beaten whites on top and fold in gently until no streaks of white or yellow remain. Now fold in the whipped cream the same way. Chill the mousse at least 3 hours or until softly set, then spoon into dessert goblets and serve, garnished, if you like, with jaunty sprigs of lemon verbena. 131 calories per serving.

COOL CRANBERRY MOUSSE WITH DRAMBUIE

Serves 8

I think this is a perfectly splendid choice for Thanksgiving or Christmas dessert. The mousse is properly festive but light, a welcome change from a heavy holiday meal.

2 cups fresh or frozen cranberries, washed, sorted and stemmed
½ cup water
3 tablespoons Drambuie
  Juice of 1 large orange
  Juice of 1 large lemon
1 envelope plus 1½ teaspoons plain gelatin
4 large eggs, separated
  Rind of 1 large orange, grated very fine
¼ teaspoon finely grated lemon rind
14 packets (1 gram each) aspartame sweetener
⅛ teaspoon salt
4 tablespoons superfine sugar
½ cup ice-cold evaporated skim milk, whipped to stiff peaks

Place the cranberries and water in a small heavy saucepan, cover, set over moderately low heat and simmer 15 minutes until the skins have popped and the berries are soft. Mix in the Drambuie, then puree by buzzing in an electric blender at high speed or in a food processor fitted with the metal chopping blade or by forcing through a food mill. Sieve the puree to remove skins and seeds; place the cranberry puree in a large heatproof bowl and set aside.

Pour the orange and lemon juices into a small, heavy pan (preferably stainless steel, flameproof glass or enameled cast iron so that the sauce doesn't take on a metallic taste) and sprinkle the gelatin evenly over the surface; let stand 5 minutes. Set over moderately low heat and cook, whisking constantly, for

3 to 4 minutes until the gelatin has completely dissolved. Beat the egg yolks lightly, whisk in a little of the hot orange mixture, stir back into pan, turn heat to its lowest point and cook and stir about 1 minute or until no raw egg taste remains. Remove from the heat and whisk into the cranberry mixture along with the orange and lemon rinds.

Set in an ice bath and whisk until the mixture reaches room temperature; blend in the sweetener, then continue whisking until thick and syrupy. Beat the egg whites with the salt until frothy, add 1 tablespoon of the sugar and beat until silvery. Continue beating the egg whites, adding the remaining sugar, a tablespoon at a time, until they peak stiffly. Blend about $\frac{1}{2}$ cup of the whites into the mousse mixture to lighten it, then gently fold in the remaining whites until no streaks of white or red remain. Now fold in the whipped evaporated skim milk the same way. Chill the mousse at least 3 hours or until softly set, then spoon into dessert goblets and serve, garnished, if you like, with sprigs of mint. 125 calories per serving.

RUM-PEACH REFRIGERATOR MOUSSE
Serves 8

For all its richness, this gelatin mousse is astonishingly low in calories because its foundation is pure pureed peaches. It's important that you choose *tree*-ripened peaches for proper flavor, not those that have been picked green and shipped cross-country. Serve the mousse as is, or splurge on a few extra calories and top with a little Peach Grand Marnier Sauce.

$\frac{1}{2}$ cup water
2 envelopes plain gelatin
8 very ripe peaches, peeled, pitted, pureed and sieved
   Juice of 1 large lemon
$\frac{1}{4}$ teaspoon finely grated orange rind
$\frac{1}{4}$ teaspoon ground mace
2 large egg yolks, lightly beaten
1 tablespoon dark rum
$\frac{1}{2}$ teaspoon almond extract
10 packets (1 gram each) aspartame sweetener
1 cup ice-cold evaporated milk

Place the water in a medium-size heavy saucepan, sprinkle the gelatin evenly over the surface and let stand 5 minutes. Add the peach puree, all but 1 tablespoon of the lemon juice, the orange rind and mace. Set over moderate heat and stir 4 to 5 minutes, just until steam rises from the surface. Whisk a little of the hot mixture into the beaten egg yolks, stir back into pan and cook and stir about 1 minute; don't allow to boil or the mixture may curdle. Remove from the heat, pour into a large heatproof bowl and set in an ice bath. Whisk often until mixture cools to room temperature—5 to 10 minutes. Stir in the rum, almond extract and sweetener. Continue to whisk the mixture until it begins to thicken—it should be about the consistency of mayonnaise. This will take 10 to 15 minutes.

Whip the evaporated milk with the reserved tablespoon of

lemon juice to stiff peaks, then fold into the peach mixture until no streaks of white or orange remain. Chill about 1 hour before serving or until softly set. Spoon into goblets, trim with a fresh peach slice and a sprig of lemon verbena, and serve. Or top, if you like, with a tablespoon or two of Peach Grand Marnier Sauce (see p. 170). 126 calories per serving; add 19 calories for each tablespoon of Peach Grand Marnier Sauce used.

SILKY CHOCOLATE MOUSSE
Serves 8

I like this decalorized mousse almost as much as the extravagant French original with its avalanche of whipped cream.

    5 tablespoons cocoa powder (not a mix)
    2 tablespoons cornstarch
    1 envelope plain gelatin
    1 cup evaporated skim milk
    ¼ cup skim milk
    4 large eggs, separated
    12 packets (1 gram each) aspartame sweetener
    2 teaspoons vanilla
    ⅛ teaspoon salt
    4 tablespoons superfine sugar
    ½ cup ice-cold evaporated milk (there should be plenty
        of ice crystals in the milk)

Combine the cocoa powder, cornstarch and gelatin in a small heavy saucepan, pressing out all lumps. Whisk in the evaporated skim milk and skim milk, then beat in the egg yolks until mixture is smooth.

NOTE: If you have a food processor, equip it with the metal chopping blade, then buzz the cocoa powder, cornstarch and gelatin (you'll have to seal the feed tube with a piece of paper toweling to keep the cocoa and cornstarch dust from flying out); add the two milks and egg yolks and buzz briefly until smooth, then dump into a small heavy saucepan. The advantage of using the processor is that it mixes up everything so quickly and completely that there's little chance of the sauce's separating as it cooks.

Set the saucepan over moderately low heat and stir vigorously for 4 to 5 minutes until thickened and smooth (do not boil or the mixture may curdle). Remove from the heat, transfer to a heatproof bowl and set in an ice bath. Whisk constantly until the mixture has cooled to room temperature; beat in the sweetener and vanilla, then continue whisking in the ice bath until the mixture is very thick and syrupy. This will take anywhere from

5 to 10 to 15 minutes, depending upon whether the bowl is metal or pottery. Beat the egg whites with the salt until frothy; add 1 tablespoon of the sugar and beat until silvery, then continue adding the sugar, 1 tablespoon at a time, beating all the while until the whites form stiff peaks when you withdraw the beater.

Mix about $\frac{1}{2}$ cup of the beaten whites into the chocolate mixture to lighten it. Now gently fold the balance of the beaten whites into the chocolate mixture until no streaks of white or brown remain (work with the bowl of mousse in the ice bath). Now whip the evaporated milk to very stiff peaks.

NOTE: You will find that the milk whips much more quickly if the bowl and beaters are also ice-cold. I pour the milk into a metal bowl and stick it into the freezer until it is about half frozen and I chill the beaters in the freezer for the same length of time.

Fold the whipped milk into the chocolate, again using a gentle touch. Chill, uncovered, for about 2 hours, then lighten the mixture by folding through it with a rubber spatula 8 to 10 times; this also rumples the surface of the mousse and makes it more attractive. You can at this point transfer the mousse to a crystal serving dish or spoon into individual goblets. Chill another 2 to 3 hours before serving. 138 calories per serving.

COOL LIME-AND-MANGO SOUFFLÉ
Serves 8

Exotic and different!

NOTE: Don't attempt to make this recipe with mangoes that are less than completely ripe (they should feel soft and smell of ambrosia) because the soufflé will have a bitter aftertaste. You will also find that the mango flesh clings so tenaciously to the pit that you will lose a good bit of it.

$\frac{1}{2}$ cup water
1 envelope plus 2 teaspoons plain gelatin
2 large (about 1 pound each) mangoes
  Juice of 2 large limes
$\frac{1}{4}$ teaspoon finely grated lime rind
3 large eggs, separated
4 packets (1 gram each) aspartame sweetener
$\frac{1}{2}$ cup ice-cold evaporated milk
1 tablespoon lemon juice
  Pinch salt
4 tablespoons superfine sugar

Place the water in a medium-size heavy saucepan, sprinkle the gelatin evenly over the surface and let stand 5 minutes. Meanwhile, halve and pit the mangoes. Scoop the flesh into a food processor fitted with the metal chopping blade or into an electric blender cup, add the lime juice and rind and puree, using two to three 30-second churnings and scraping the sides of the work bowl or blender cup down between each with a rubber spatula.

NOTE: If you have neither food processor nor blender, force the mango flesh through a food mill, then mix in the lime juice and rind. Press the puree through a fine sieve to remove any fibers (with which mangoes seem abundantly blessed).

Mix the mango mixture into the gelatin, set over moderate heat and stir 4 to 5 minutes, just until steam rises from the surface. Beat the egg yolks until frothy, whisk in a little of the

71

hot mango mixture, stir back into pan and whisk and stir about 1 minute—just long enough to cook the egg yolks. Do not permit the mixture to boil or it may curdle.

Remove from the heat, pour into a large heatproof bowl, set in an ice bath and whisk often until the mixture cools to room temperature—5 to 10 minutes. Stir in the sweetener and continue whisking until the mixture thickens to the consistency of mayonnaise—10 to 15 minutes.

Whip the evaporated milk with the lemon juice to stiff peaks, then fold into the mango mixture until no streaks of white or yellow remain. Now beat the egg whites with the salt until frothy, add 1 tablespoon of the sugar and beat until silvery. Continue beating the egg whites vigorously, adding the remaining sugar, 1 tablespoon at a time, until the whites stand in stiff peaks. Dump on top of the mango mixture and fold in gently but thoroughly with a rubber spatula.

Pour the mixture into an ungreased 6-cup soufflé dish and chill 4 to 5 hours until softly set. Dish up and serve topped by twists of lime. 180 calories per serving.

BAKED ORANGE CUSTARDS
Serves 6

If these custards are to be properly silky, bake them in a water bath, which will minimize the possibility of their curdling.

1 cup evaporated skim milk
1 cup milk
3 large eggs
2 tablespoons light brown sugar
2 tablespoons granulated sugar
1 tablespoon Grand Marnier
$\frac{1}{4}$ teaspoon finely grated orange rind
$\frac{1}{4}$ teaspoon almond extract
   Light sprinklings of ground mace

Place the evaporated skim milk and milk in a medium-size heavy saucepan, set over moderate heat and bring just to the scalding point (steam will rise from the milk but the surface of the milk will not tremble or bubble). Meanwhile, beat the eggs with the light brown and granulated sugars, the Grand Marnier, orange rind and almond extract in a medium-size heatproof bowl. Pour in the hot milk and stir to mix.

Pour into 6 ungreased 6-ounce custard cups, sprinkle each lightly with mace and set in a large shallow baking pan. Pour water into the baking pan to a depth of 1″, then bake the custards in a moderately slow oven (325°F.) for about 45 minutes or until a silver knife inserted into a custard midway between the center and the edge comes out clean. Remove the custards from the oven and from the water bath, cool to room temperature, then chill several hours before serving. 136 calories per serving.

POTS DE CRÈME AU CHOCOLAT
Serves 6

Surprisingly dark and rich.

 5 tablespoons cocoa powder (not a mix)
 2 tablespoons cornstarch
 1 teaspoon plain gelatin
 1 cup evaporated skim milk
 1½ cups skim milk
 3 large egg yolks, lightly beaten
 10 packets (1 gram each) aspartame sweetener
 2 teaspoons vanilla
 3 tablespoons heavy cream

In a small heavy saucepan combine the cocoa, cornstarch and gelatin, pressing out all lumps; whisk in the evaporated skim milk and skim milk. When mixture is absolutely uniform and no flecks of dry cocoa or cornstarch remain, set over moderately low heat and stir 3 to 4 minutes, just until mixture bubbles up and thickens. Whisk a little of the hot mixture into the egg yolks, stir back into the pan, and heat and stir 1 minute; do not allow the mixture to boil at this point or it may curdle.

Remove from the heat and cool to room temperature, whisking often to prevent a skin from forming on the surface of the sauce. Mix in the sweetener, vanilla and heavy cream, pour into six 4-ounce *pots de crème* or ramekins and chill 3 to 4 hours until softly set. Cover snugly with plastic food wrap and keep refrigerated. When serving, top, if you like, with small dollops of Crème Chantilly (see p. 178). 155 calories per serving; add 5 calories for each tablespoon of Crème Chantilly.

OEUFS À LA NEIGE
Serves 6

This is a pastry-cart staple at fashionable French restaurants, slimmed down for dieters. The trick in making the "snow eggs" is to poach the meringue just until set—no more, no less. Under-poached meringues may separate (weep) on standing or, worse yet, disintegrate, and overpoached ones may toughen (and also weep).

  2 cups milk
  1 cup skim milk
  2 large vanilla beans, split lengthwise
  3 large egg whites
  $\frac{1}{8}$ teaspoon salt
  6 tablespoons superfine sugar
  4 large egg yolks, lightly beaten
  1 large egg, lightly beaten
  10 packets (1 gram each) aspartame sweetener

Place the milk, skim milk and vanilla beans in a large, shallow, heavy saucepan and set over moderately low heat (you will poach the meringues in the milk, then use the milk for the stirred custard on which you will later float them). Beat the egg whites with the salt until frothy, add 1 tablespoon of the sugar and beat until silvery; add the remaining sugar, 1 tablespoon at a time, beating all the while. As soon as the egg whites form stiff peaks when you withdraw the beater, they are ready to shape. Set a glass of cold water on the counter beside the stove, then dip in 2 tablespoons. Take up a mound of meringue on one table-spoon, then sculpt into a plump egg with the other tablespoon and slide gently into the simmering milk. The milk, by the way, should never boil, just tremble slightly. Continue shaping the remaining meringue the same way, dipping the tablespoons often in the cold water to prevent sticking. Poach the meringues for 2 minutes in the hot milk, turn and poach 2 minutes longer, then lift to a wet tray to cool. Continue shaping and poaching the snow eggs until all of the meringue is used up.

Strain the milk into a clean, heavy saucepan; scrape the seeds out of the vanilla pods into the milk; discard the pods. Combine the beaten yolks and the egg, whisk in a little of the hot milk, stir back into pan, set over low heat and cook, stirring constantly, just until the custard thickens and no longer tastes of raw egg. At no time permit the custard to boil because it will curdle. If the custard should curdle despite all precautions, simply pour it through a fine sieve. Cool to room temperature, whisking often to prevent a skin from forming on the surface; then blend in the sweetener.

Pour the custard into a broad-bottomed crystal bowl, float the poached meringues on top, then chill several hours before serving. 180 calories per serving.

GINGER ROOT SOUFFLÉ
Serves 4

Deliciously different!

NOTE: Whenever you make a soufflé, use the freshest eggs possible. Stale whites will not whip properly and may break down when you attempt to fold them into the soufflé base. The whites of absolutely fresh eggs will mound slightly when you break them into a bowl; stale eggs are runny and will flatten out.

For Preparing the Soufflé Dish:

1 generous spraying of nonstick vegetable cooking spray
4 teaspoons sugar

The Soufflé Mixture:

2 tablespoons plus 1 teaspoon cornstarch
7 tablespoons sugar
½ teaspoon ground ginger
¼ teaspoon ground nutmeg
¾ cup milk
3 large egg yolks, lightly beaten
3 tablespoons very finely minced preserved ginger
    (measure firmly packed)
¼ teaspoon finely grated lemon rind
5 large egg whites
¼ teaspoon salt

Prepare the Soufflé Dish First: Spray generously the bottom and sides of a 2½-quart soufflé dish with the nonstick vegetable cooking spray, dump in the sugar and tilt the dish from one side to another until the bottom and sides of the dish are evenly coated with sugar; tap out any excess sugar. Set the dish aside.

For the Soufflé: In a small heavy saucepan, combine the cornstarch, 3 tablespoons of the sugar, the ginger and nutmeg, pressing out any lumps. Whisk in the milk, set over moderately low heat and whisk constantly 3 to 4 minutes until thickened and translucent; the mixture will be quite stiff. Whisk a little of the hot mixture into the egg yolks, stir back into pan, turn heat down low and whisk about 1 minute, just until no raw egg flavor remains. Remove from the heat, pour into a large mixing bowl, mix in the preserved ginger and lemon rind and cool to room temperature.

Beat the egg whites with the salt until frothy; add 1 tablespoon of the remaining sugar and beat until frothy. Now add the remaining 3 tablespoons of sugar, 1 tablespoon at a time, beating all the while. When all of the sugar has been incorporated, continue beating the whites until glossy and stiff but not dry. Stir about one-third of the beaten whites into the ginger mixture, then dump the remaining whites on top and fold in gently but thoroughly until no streaks of white or yellow remain.

Pour the soufflé mixture into the prepared dish and bake in a moderate oven (350°F.) 30 to 35 minutes or until the soufflé is puffed, browned on top but still soft enough inside to quiver when you nudge the dish. Hurry the soufflé to the table and serve. 255 calories per serving.

FRESH PEACH SOUFFLÉ

Serves 4

The very essence of summer.

NOTE: The flavor of this fragile soufflé will be only as good as the peaches you use because, greatly reduced, they form the foundation of the soufflé— there are no egg yolks or starch to thicken the mixture. So make certain that the peaches you choose are tree-ripened and at the peak of their flavor.

For Preparing the Soufflé Dish:

1 teaspoon unsalted butter
4 teaspoons sugar

The Soufflé Mixture:

3 cups peeled, pitted, sliced ripe peaches (you'll need 5 to 6 medium-size peaches)
$\frac{1}{4}$ cup water
1 vanilla bean, split
2 tablespoons peach jam
2 teaspoons lemon juice
1 tablespoon peach brandy or Grand Marnier
$\frac{1}{4}$ teaspoon almond extract
4 large egg whites, at room temperature
$\frac{1}{4}$ teaspoon salt
2 tablespoons sugar

Prepare the Soufflé Dish First: Butter a 6-cup soufflé dish well, add the sugar and coat the bottom and sides of the dish evenly by tilting the dish from one side to another. Tap out the excess. Chill the dish at least 30 minutes before you use it.

For the Soufflé: Place the peaches, water and vanilla bean in a medium-size heavy saucepan (not aluminum, which may give the peaches a metallic taste), set over moderate heat and bring to a boil; adjust the heat underneath the peaches so that they bubble gently; simmer uncovered, stirring often, for 1 hour or until the peaches have reduced to 1 cup. Remove and discard the vanilla bean, then puree the peaches by buzzing in a food processor fitted with the metal chopping blade, in an electric blender at high speed or by forcing through a food mill. Mix in the jam, lemon juice, peach brandy and almond extract.

Beat the egg whites with the salt to soft peaks, then slowly add the sugar, 1 tablespoon at a time, beating all the while. Continue beating the whites until stiff but not dry. Stir about one-third of the whites into the peach base to lighten it, then fold in the remaining whites gently but thoroughly until no streaks of white or orange remain.

Pour the soufflé mixture into the prepared soufflé dish and bake in a moderately hot oven (375°F.) for 30 to 35 minutes until puffed and brown. Rush to the table and serve as is or accompanied by Peach Grand Marnier Sauce (see p. 170). 148 calories per serving: add 19 calories for each tablespoon of Peach Grand Marnier Sauce used.

GRAND MARNIER SOUFFLÉ
Serves 4

Exquisite orange flavor.

For Preparing the Soufflé Dish:

1 generous spraying of nonstick vegetable cooking spray
4 teaspoons sugar

The Soufflé Mixture:

2 tablespoons cornstarch
7 tablespoons sugar
¾ cup freshly squeezed orange juice
2 tablespoons Grand Marnier
4 large egg yolks, lightly beaten
1 tablespoon finely grated orange rind
2 packets (1 gram each) aspartame sweetener
5 large egg whites
¼ teaspoon salt

Prepare the Soufflé Dish First: Spray generously the bottom and sides of a 2-quart soufflé dish with the nonstick vegetable cooking spray, dump in the sugar and tilt the dish from one side to another until the bottom and sides of the dish are evenly coated with sugar; tap out any excess sugar. Set the dish aside.

For the Soufflé: In a small heavy saucepan, combine the cornstarch and 3 tablespoons of the sugar, pressing out all lumps. Stir in the orange juice and Grand Marnier, set over moderately low heat and whisk constantly 3 to 4 minutes until the mixture bubbles up, thickens and clears; it will be quite stiff. Whisk a little of the hot mixture into the egg yolks, stir back into pan, turn heat down low and whisk about 1 minute, just until no raw egg flavor remains. Remove from the heat, pour into a large mixing bowl and cool to room temperature. Mix in the orange rind and sweetener.

NOTE: You can make the soufflé base well ahead of time; simply place a piece of plastic food wrap flat on the surface of the cooled orange mixture and place in the refrigerator; let stand at room temperature about 30 minutes before folding in the egg whites.

Beat the egg whites with the salt until frothy; add 1 tablespoon of the remaining sugar and beat until frothy. Now add the remaining 3 tablespoons of sugar, 1 tablespoon at a time, beating all the while. When all of the sugar has been incorporated, continue beating the whites until glossy and stiff but not dry. Stir about one-third of the beaten whites into the orange mixture, then dump the remaining whites on top and fold in gently but thoroughly until no streaks of white or orange remain.

Pour the soufflé mixture into the prepared dish and bake in a moderate oven (350°F.) about 40 minutes or until the soufflé is puffed, browned on top but still soft enough inside to quiver when you nudge the dish. Rush the soufflé to the table and serve. 226 calories per serving.

FRESH GRAPEFRUIT SOUFFLÉ
Serves 4

Because I'm partial to grapefruit, I worked out this recipe. The grated rind injects pungent grapefruit flavor.

For Preparing the Soufflé Dish:

    1 generous spraying of nonstick vegetable cooking spray
    4 teaspoons sugar

The Soufflé Mixture:

    2 tablespoons cornstarch
    7 tablespoons sugar
    $\frac{3}{4}$ cup freshly squeezed grapefruit juice
    4 large egg yolks, lightly beaten
    1 tablespoon finely grated grapefruit rind
    3 packets (1 gram each) aspartame sweetener
    5 large egg whites
    $\frac{1}{4}$ teaspoon salt

Prepare the Soufflé Dish First: Spray the bottom and sides of a 2-quart soufflé dish generously with nonstick vegetable cooking spray, dump in the sugar and tilt the dish from one side to another until the bottom and sides are evenly coated with sugar. Tap out any excess sugar; set the dish aside.

For the Soufflé: In a small heavy saucepan, combine the cornstarch and 3 tablespoons of the sugar, pressing out any lumps. Stir in the grapefruit juice, set over moderately low heat and whisk constantly 3 to 4 minutes until the mixture bubbles up, thickens and clears; it will be quite stiff. Whisk a little of the hot grapefruit mixture into the egg yolks, stir back into the pan, turn heat down low and whisk about 1 minute, just until no raw egg flavor remains. Remove from the heat, transfer to a large mixing bowl and cool to room temperature. Mix in the grapefruit rind and sweetener.

NOTE: You can make the grapefruit soufflé base well ahead of time; simply place a piece of plastic food wrap flat on the surface of the cooled mixture and place in the refrigerator; let stand at room temperature about 30 minutes before folding in the egg whites.

Beat the egg whites with the salt until frothy; add 1 tablespoon of the remaining sugar and beat until frothy. Now add the remaining 3 tablespoons of sugar, 1 tablespoon at a time, beating all the while. When all of the sugar has been incorporated, continue beating the whites until glossy and stiff but not dry. Stir about one-third of the beaten whites into the grapefruit mixture, then dump the remaining whites on top and fold in gently but thoroughly until no streaks of white or yellow remain.

Pour the soufflé mixture into the prepared dish and bake in a moderate oven (350°F.) about 40 minutes or until the soufflé is puffed, browned on top but still soft enough inside to quiver when you nudge the dish. Rush the soufflé to the table and serve. 208 calories per serving.

DARK CHOCOLATE SOUFFLÉ
Serves 4

When perfectly cooked, this soufflé will be crusty on the outside but as quivery and moist as a mousse when you cut into it. Waste no time serving the soufflé because it will deflate once it's taken from the oven.

For Preparing the Soufflé Dish:

> 1 generous spraying of nonstick vegetable cooking spray
> 4 teaspoons sugar

The Soufflé Mixture:

> 2 tablespoons cornstarch
> 4 tablespoons cocoa powder (not a mix)
> 1 cup milk
> 4 large egg yolks, lightly beaten
> 10 packets (1 gram each) aspartame sweetener
> $1\frac{1}{2}$ teaspoons vanilla
> 5 large egg whites
> $\frac{1}{4}$ teaspoon salt
> 4 tablespoons sugar

Prepare the Soufflé Dish First: Spray the bottom and sides of a 2-quart soufflé dish generously with the nonstick vegetable cooking spray, dump in the sugar and coat the dish well by tilting it from one side to another; make sure that the sides are well coated with sugar, too. Tap out any excess sugar; set the dish aside.

For the Soufflé: In a shaker jar with a tight-fitting lid or in a food processor fitted with the metal chopping blade, combine the cornstarch, cocoa and milk by shaking or whirring vigorously; there should be no lumps and no traces of dry cocoa or cornstarch. Pour into a small heavy saucepan, set over moderately low heat and whisk constantly for 3 to 4 minutes, just until the mixture thickens and clears; it will be very thick. Blend a little of the chocolate mixture into the egg yolks, stir back into pan, turn heat to its lowest point and whisk vigorously for about 1 minute or until no raw egg taste lingers. Remove the chocolate mixture from the heat, pour into a large mixing bowl and cool to room temperature, beating often to prevent a skin from forming on the surface of the sauce. Blend in the sweetener and vanilla.

NOTE: You can accelerate the cooling by setting the bowl of chocolate mixture in an ice bath and whisking hard. You can also make the soufflé up to this point well ahead of time. Simply place a piece of plastic food wrap flat on the surface of the cooled mixture and keep refrigerated until about 30 minutes before you are ready to bake the soufflé; let the sauce stand on the counter 30 minutes before folding in the egg whites.

Beat the egg whites with the salt until frothy; add 1 tablespoon of the sugar and beat until frothy. Now add the remaining sugar, 1 tablespoon at a time, beating all the while. When all of the sugar has been incorporated, continue beating the whites until glossy and stiff but not dry. Blend about one-third of the whites into the chocolate mixture (this is to lighten it and facilitate folding in the balance of the whites). Dump the remaining whites on top of the chocolate mixture and fold in gently but thoroughly until no streaks of white or brown remain.

Pour the soufflé mixture into the prepared soufflé dish and bake in a moderately hot oven (375°F.) 35 to 40 minutes until puffed, browned on top but still soft enough inside to quiver when you nudge the dish. Rush the soufflé to the table and serve. 230 calories per serving.

MULLED WINE JELLY
Serves 6

This recipe evolved out of an attempt to save the poaching liquid from Burgundy-Poached Pears, and it's delicious if I do say so myself. Of course, you can begin from scratch, if you like (I offer both methods below). This is a spicy, softly set jelly that's prettiest when mounded into stemmed goblets and trickled with a little cream or Crème Anglaise.

2 cups dry red wine
    (preferably a Burgundy
    type)
2 cups water
    Juice of $\frac{1}{2}$ lemon
$\frac{1}{2}$ cinnamon stick
1 envelope plus 1 teaspoon
    plain gelatin
    Juice of 1 large orange
6 packets (1 gram each)
    aspartame sweetener

or instead of these first 4 ingredients, use 1 quart strained poaching liquid from Burgundy-Poached Pears (see p. 111).

If You Are Beginning the Recipe from Scratch: Place the wine, water, lemon juice and cinnamon in a heavy enameled or stainless steel saucepan, set over moderate heat and allow to steep just below the simmering point for 15 minutes; stir occasionally. Meanwhile, soak the gelatin in the orange juice. When the wine has mulled 15 minutes, discard the cinnamon. Stir in the gelatin mixture and warm 2 to 3 minutes, just until completely dissolved. Cool to room temperature, stir in the sweetener, then pour into a glass bowl, cover and chill overnight until softly set.

If You Are Using the Poaching Liquid: Measure the poaching liquid carefully; if there is not quite 1 quart, round out the measure with a little additional wine or water. Pour into a glass bowl. Soften the gelatin in the orange juice 2 to 3 minutes in a small heavy saucepan, then set over moderately low heat and stir 3 to 4 minutes until gelatin is completely dissolved; stir into the wine mixture along with the sweetener. Cover and chill overnight until softly set.

To serve, spoon into stemmed goblets and trickle, if you like, with a little half-and-half cream or Crème Anglaise (see p. 165). 91 calories per serving without any topping; add 16 calories for each tablespoon of Crème Anglaise used and 20 calories for each tablespoon of half-and-half.

3
FROZEN DESSERTS

VANILLA BEAN ICE CREAM
Serves 6

The problem in making ice cream with little heavy cream (or no heavy cream at all) is that it will be granular. It is the butterfat in the ice cream that separates and minimizes the ice crystals. How to create the same effect without sabotaging the calorie count involves food chemistry and physics. What is needed are low-calorie stabilizers—"smoother-outers," if you will. I have used two—cornstarch and eggs, both of which help to make the ice cream creamy without rocketing the calorie content out of reason. In fact, the calorie count of the ice cream base was so low that I was able to add ½ cup of heavy cream.

NOTE: Because of this ice cream's low butterfat content, it's essential that you beat it hard—several times—when it has frozen to the mushy stage. What you are doing is breaking the ice crystals down mechanically. If you have a food processor, you can whir the ice cream to pure satin with no effort at all.

> 2 tablespoons cornstarch
> 2 tablespoons sugar
> 2 cups milk
> 2 cups skim milk
> 3 large egg yolks, lightly beaten
> 1 large egg, lightly beaten
> 2 large vanilla beans, split lengthwise
> 10 packets (1 gram each) aspartame sweetener
> ½ cup heavy cream, whipped to soft peaks

Combine the cornstarch and sugar in a medium-size heavy saucepan, pressing out all lumps; stir in the milk and skim milk, beat in the egg yolks and egg, then drop in the vanilla beans. Set over moderately low heat and cook, stirring constantly, 4 to 5 minutes until the consistency of custard sauce. Do not allow to boil or the sauce may curdle. Remove from the heat and cool to lukewarm, whisking often to prevent a skin from forming on the surface of the sauce. Remove and discard the vanilla beans, then blend in the sweetener.

Pour the ice cream base into a 13″ x 9″ x 2″ pan and freeze until mushy firm. Beat at highest mixer speed (or in a food processor fitted with the metal chopping blade) until fluffy light. Fold in the whipped cream, return to the pan and freeze until mushy firm. Again beat until fluffy light, freeze until soft-firm and serve.

NOTE: Always let this ice cream soften slightly before you serve it, particularly if it should become brick hard. 154 calories per serving.

Variation:

Grenadian Fresh Nutmeg Ice Cream: Make the custard base as directed, but use 1 vanilla bean only. As soon as the base has reached the proper consistency, remove it from the heat, fish out and discard the vanilla bean. Now mix in 1 freshly grated nutmeg.

NOTE: You must use freshly grated nutmeg, not the commercially ground, which will give the ice cream an unpleasant bitter taste. From this point on, proceed precisely as the recipe directs above. 154 calories per serving.

FRENCH CHOCOLATE ICE CREAM
Serves 8

This ice cream is best when served slightly soft. I usually let it stand 5 to 10 minutes at room temperature before I dish it up.

  6 tablespoons cocoa powder (not a mix)
  2 tablespoons cornstarch
  3 tablespoons sugar
  1 cup buttermilk
  1 can (13 ounces) evaporated skim milk
  2 large egg yolks, lightly beaten
10 packets (1 gram each) aspartame sweetener
  2 teaspoons vanilla
  1 cup nonfat dry milk powder
  1 cup ice water
  1 teaspoon lemon juice

Combine the cocoa, cornstarch and sugar in a small heavy saucepan, pressing out all lumps. Stir in the buttermilk and evaporated skim milk, set over moderately low heat and whisk 3 to 4 minutes until the mixture bubbles up and thickens. Whisk a little of the hot mixture into the egg yolks, stir back into pan and cook and stir 1 minute; do not allow to boil or the mixture may curdle. Remove from the heat and cool to room temperature, whisking often to prevent a skin from forming on the surface of the sauce. Mix in the sweetener and vanilla, pour into a 13" x 9" x 2" pan and freeze until mushy firm.

Place the nonfat dry milk powder in largest mixer bowl, pour in the ice water and stir to mix. Now whip to soft peaks by beating at highest mixer speed; add the lemon juice and continue beating until very stiff (this will take several minutes).

Now beat the chocolate mixture until fluffy light; fold in the whipped "cream," return to pan and freeze until soft-firm. Again beat until fluffy light, then freeze until firm. 163 calories per serving.

RIPE STRAWBERRY ICE CREAM
Serves 8

American strawberries, alas, appear to be going the way of American tomatoes, which is to say that they are big, beautiful and tasteless. I urge you to use vine-ripened strawberries at their peak of flavor for this recipe; otherwise the ice cream will be bland and boring. If you have a food processor, you'll find this ice cream a breeze to make.

  1 envelope plain gelatin
  2 cups milk
  2 large eggs, beaten until frothy
  1½ pints fully ripe strawberries, washed, hulled and pureed
  12 packets (1 gram each) aspartame sweetener
  2 tablespoons lemon juice
  ¼ cup heavy cream

Sprinkle the gelatin over the milk in a small heavy saucepan, set over moderately low heat and heat and stir 3 to 4 minutes until gelatin dissolves completely. In a food processor fitted with the metal chopping blade, buzz the eggs 2 to 3 seconds. Then with the motor running, drizzle the milk-gelatin mixture down the feed tube; cool to room temperature. With motor running, spoon the strawberries down the feed tube; buzz until smooth and creamy, then add the sweetener and lemon juice and whir until incorporated.

Pour into a 13″ x 9″ x 2″ pan and freeze until mushy. Beat the ice cream until fluffy in the food processor (or in an electric mixer at high speed). Beat in the cream. Return all to pan, freeze until mushy and again beat until fluffy. Freeze until soft-firm and serve as is or topped by fresh sliced strawberries. 115 calories per serving; add 25 calories for each ½ cup unsweetened sliced strawberries.

SILKY AVOCADO ICE CREAM
Serves 8

So elegant, so easy (if you have a food processor) and so refreshing. You can tint the ice cream pale yellow green, if you like, but I prefer not to because I like the subtlety of the avocado's natural color.

   2 large ripe avocados
     Juice of 2 lemons
     Juice of 1 orange
     Finely grated rind of 1 lemon
  10 packets (1 gram each) aspartame sweetener
   1 can (13 ounces) evaporated skim milk
     Pinch ground ginger
     Pinch ground mace
     Pinch ground cinnamon
   $\frac{1}{2}$ teaspoon almond extract
   1 cup ice-cold evaporated milk

Halve the avocados, discard pits, then scoop the avocado flesh directly into the work bowl of a food processor fitted with the metal chopping blade (or drop into an electric blender cup). Reserve 1 tablespoon of the lemon juice (you will use it in whipping the evaporated milk later); dump the balance of the lemon juice over the avocados and buzz until smooth—about four 30-second churnings of the motor should be about right.

NOTE: If you have neither processor nor blender, force the avocados through a food mill and mix at once with the lemon juice. Beat in the orange juice and lemon rind, the sweetener, evaporated skim milk, ginger, mace, cinnamon and almond extract. Pour into a 13″ x 9″ x 2″ pan and freeze several hours until mushy firm. Pour the ice-cold evaporated milk into the bowl in which you'll whip it and set both it and the beater in the freezer (having the milk, bowl and beater ice-cold makes the evaporated milk whip much more quickly and dramatically).

   When the ice cream is mushy firm, dump into the largest

mixer bowl and beat at high speed until fluffy light. Also whip the ice-cold evaporated milk with the 1 tablespoon of reserved lemon juice to stiff peaks. Fold the whipped milk into the avocado mixture, return to the pan and freeze until soft-firm. Dish up and serve. 190 calories per serving.

BANANA-NUTMEG ICE CREAM
Serves 10

Sheer velvet, and yet there's not an ounce of cream in this low-calorie version of an "ice cream" I once enjoyed on the West Indian island of Grenada.

NOTE: You must use freshly grated nutmeg for this recipe, not the commercially ground, which will taste bitter if used in this quantity.

> 4 medium-size *very ripe* bananas
> Juice of 1 large lemon
> Juice of 2 large oranges
> Rind of 1 large orange, grated fine
> 1 can (13 ounces) evaporated skim milk
> 8 packets (1 gram each) aspartame sweetener
> ¾ teaspoon almond extract
> ½ teaspoon *freshly grated* nutmeg
> 1 cup ice-cold evaporated milk

Peel the bananas, remove strings, then slice directly into a food processor work bowl fitted with the metal chopping blade (or drop into an electric blender cup). Reserve 1 tablespoon of the lemon juice to use in whipping the evaporated milk; dump the balance over the banana slices and buzz until smooth—about four 30-second churnings of the motor.

NOTE: If you have neither processor nor blender, you can beat the bananas with the lemon juice until smooth using an electric mixer set at high speed. Beat in the orange juice and rind, the evaporated skim milk, the sweetener, almond extract and nutmeg. Pour into a 13″ x 9″ x 2″ pan and freeze several hours until mushy firm. Pour the ice-cold evaporated milk into the bowl in which you intend to whip it and set in the freezer along with the beater.

When the ice cream is mushy firm, dump into largest mixer bowl and beat at high speed until fluffy. Also whip the ice-cold evaporated milk with the reserved 1 tablespoon of lemon juice to stiff peaks. Fold the whipped milk into the banana mixture, return to the pan and freeze until soft-firm. Dish up and serve. 126 calories per serving.

CHAMPAGNE SHERBET
Serves 6

The champagne you use for this recipe should be full-bodied, moderately dry and not too expensive. I use a favorite California label that doesn't cost the earth.

1 cup water
1 envelope plain gelatin
¼ cup lemon juice
   Rind of 1 large lemon, grated fine
1 bottle (750 milliliters or 25.4 fluid ounces) dry
   champagne
10 packets (1 gram each) aspartame sweetener

Place the water in a small heavy saucepan, sprinkle the gelatin over the surface and let stand 5 minutes; set over moderate heat and stir 3 to 4 minutes until the gelatin dissolves completely. Pour into a large heatproof bowl, stir in the lemon juice and rind and cool to room temperature. Mix in the champagne and sweetener and freeze several hours until mushy firm. In an electric mixer set at high speed, beat the sherbet until fluffy light. Return to the freezer, again freeze until mushy firm and again beat until light. Freeze until soft-firm, spoon into stemmed goblets and serve. 71 calories per serving.

Variation:

Peach Coupe Champagne: In each of 6 large stemmed goblets, place a peeled and pitted very ripe peach half, hollow-side up. Cradle a generous scoop of Champagne Sherbet in each peach hollow, sprig with lemon verbena or mint and serve as a party dessert. About 100 calories per serving.

PAPAYA-PINEAPPLE SHERBET
Serves 8

A low-calorie version of a Caribbean "cooler" that I enjoyed years ago in Trinidad. It's best when it has the consistency of a frozen daiquiri.

1 small ripe papaya
1 can (1 pound 4 ounces) crushed pineapple in
    unsweetened pineapple juice (do not drain)
½ cup water
1 envelope plain gelatin
2 cups buttermilk
¼ cup fresh lime juice
6 packets (1 gram each) aspartame sweetener
½ teaspoon vanilla

Halve the papaya, scoop out and discard seeds. Spoon papaya flesh into a food processor fitted with the metal chopping blade or into an electric blender and buzz until uniformly smooth. Dump the papaya puree into a large shallow bowl, mix in the crushed pineapple and juice and set aside.

Place the water in a small heavy saucepan, sprinkle the gelatin evenly over the surface and let stand several minutes. Set over moderate heat and stir 3 to 4 minutes until the gelatin dissolves completely. Remove from the heat, cool 5 minutes, then combine with the buttermilk and stir into the pineapple mixture. Mix in the lime juice, sweetener and vanilla and freeze until mushy.

Beat the sherbet hard for 1 to 2 minutes in a food processor fitted with the metal chopping blade or in an electric mixer set at high speed. When fluffy and light, return to the freezer, freeze until mushy, then again beat until fluffy. Spoon the sherbet into a large freezer container (I use the ½-gallon size) and freeze until soft-firm. Spoon into goblets and serve. 83 calories per serving.

WATERMELON SORBET
Serves 8

Uncommonly cool and fewer calories per serving than a sliced orange.

   7 cups very ripe, seeded watermelon cubes (you'll need
       about 7 pounds of watermelon)
      Juice of 2 large limes
      Juice of 1 large lemon
  10 packets (1 gram each) aspartame sweetener
    $\frac{3}{4}$ cup water
    2 envelopes plain gelatin

Working with about half of the total amount at a time, puree the watermelon cubes in a food processor fitted with the metal chopping blade, in an electric blender at high speed or by forcing through a food mill. Combine with the lime and lemon juice and sweetener. Set aside.

Place the water in a very small heavy saucepan (a butter warmer is the perfect size), sprinkle the gelatin evenly over the surface and let stand 5 minutes. Set over low heat and stir constantly for about 4 minutes until gelatin dissolves completely. Stir gelatin into the watermelon mixture, pour into a 13" x 9" x 2" pan and freeze until mushy firm.

With an electric mixer set at high speed, beat the watermelon sorbet until light and fluffy. Freeze until mushy, beat once again until light, then freeze until soft-firm and serve. 37 calories per serving.

NOTE: For a spectacular presentation, freeze the sorbet until firm, shape into small balls with a ball scoop, then mound $\frac{1}{2}$ cup each sorbet and fresh honeydew melon balls into a stemmed goblet. About 75 calories per serving.

FRESH LIME SORBET
Serves 6

Fresh as springtime!

NOTE: Do not substitute bottled or reconstituted lime juice for the fresh because the sorbet will taste bitter.

 1 quart water
 1 envelope plain gelatin
 1 cup freshly squeezed lime juice (you'll need about 5
    large limes)
   Rind of 1 large lime, grated fine
   Juice of 1 lemon
20 packets (1 gram each) aspartame sweetener (about)
 $\frac{1}{4}$ cup light corn syrup

Place 1 cup of the water in a small heavy saucepan, sprinkle the gelatin evenly over the surface and let stand 5 minutes; set over moderate heat and stir 3 to 4 minutes until the gelatin dissolves completely. Meanwhile, place the remaining 3 cups water in a large heatproof bowl; stir in the lime juice and rind and lemon juice. As soon as the gelatin has dissolved, pour the hot mixture into the lime mixture and stir to mix. Now mix in the sweetener and corn syrup; taste the sorbet base and if it is too tart for your taste, add another packet or two of the sweetener (you'll increase the calorie count by only $\frac{2}{3}$ of a calorie per serving for each packet you add).

Freeze the lime mixture several hours until mushy firm; beat until light in an electric mixer set at high speed. Again freeze until mushy firm and beat until light. Freeze until soft-firm, spoon into frosty goblets and serve trimmed with a twist of lime and sprig of mint. 70 calories per serving.

GRAPEFRUIT GRANITÉ
Serves 8

If there's a better way to cool off on a sultry summer's day than by dipping into a frosty goblet of Grapefruit Granité, I have yet to find it. Best of all, this snowy dessert averages less than 50 calories per serving.

1 cup water
1 envelope plain gelatin
3 large grapefruits, juiced
1 tablespoon finely grated grapefruit rind
$\frac{1}{4}$ teaspoon finely grated lemon rind
10 packets (1 gram each) aspartame sweetener

Place the water in a small heavy saucepan, sprinkle the gelatin evenly over the surface and let stand 5 minutes; set over moderate heat and stir 3 to 4 minutes until the gelatin is completely dissolved. Remove from the heat. Strain the grapefruit juice into a large bowl, stir in the gelatin mixture, the grapefruit and lemon rind and sweetener. Freeze several hours until mushy firm; beat at highest mixer speed until fine and feathery, pack into a $\frac{1}{2}$-gallon plastic carton and freeze until firm.

NOTE: This granité is best if you let it thaw slightly before you serve it. 45 calories per serving.

MINTED ORANGE FREEZE
Serves 8

Heaven on a hot day!

    4 large mint sprigs, washed
    1½ cups boiling water
    1 envelope plain gelatin
    ¾ cup sugar
    2 tablespoons lemon juice
    2 teaspoons finely grated orange rind
    3 cups strained fresh orange juice

Steep the mint in the boiling water 10 minutes; strain, discarding the mint and reserving the infusion. Meanwhile, combine the gelatin and sugar in a small heavy saucepan, pressing out any lumps. Pour the mint infusion into the pan, set over moderate heat and cook and stir 3 to 5 minutes until sugar and gelatin are both dissolved. Off heat, mix in the lemon juice and orange rind. Cool to room temperature, then combine with the orange juice.

Pour into a large shallow bowl and freeze until mushy; beat until fluffy in an electric mixer set at highest speed or buzz, about half of the total amount at a time, in a food processor fitted with the metal chopping blade. Freeze again until mushy, beat until fluffy as before, then freeze until fairly firm.

Let stand at room temperature about 15 minutes before serving. Spoon into goblets and sprig, if you like, with fresh mint. 115 calories per serving.

Variation:

Tea Ice: Prepare as directed above but substitute 1½ cups freshly brewed strong tea for 1½ cups of the orange juice. 95 calories per serving.

RASPBERRY SEMIFREDDO
Serves 6

Semifreddo is Italian for "half frozen" and refers to the whole array of soft Italian ices. This one is pure velvet if you freeze it in a hand or electric freezer. But it will also be acceptably smooth if frozen in the refrigerator—*provided* you beat it at least twice just as it reaches the mushy firm stage.

 2 packages (10 ounces each) quick-thaw frozen
   raspberries
 1 cup water
 1 envelope plain gelatin
 2 tablespoons lemon juice
 ½ teaspoon finely grated orange rind
 4 packets (1 gram each) aspartame sweetener

Partially thaw the raspberries, then puree by buzzing in an electric blender at high speed or in a food processor fitted with the metal chopping blade or by forcing through a food mill. Sieve the puree to remove the seeds, place in a small mixing bowl and set aside.

Pour the water into a very small heavy saucepan, sprinkle the gelatin evenly over the surface and let stand 1 to 2 minutes; set over moderately low heat and stir 2 to 3 minutes, just until the gelatin is completely dissolved. Stir the gelatin into the raspberry puree along with the lemon juice, orange rind and sweetener.

Freeze in an ice cream maker or machine according to the manufacturer's directions. Or freeze until mushy firm in the freezing compartment of the refrigerator; with the electric mixer set at high speed, beat the raspberry mixture until fluffy light (or buzz it up in a food processor fitted with the metal chopping blade). Again freeze until mushy firm and again beat until light. Serve at once. 110 calories per serving.

FROZEN STRAWBERRY YOGURT

Serves 6

Wonderfully tart, wonderfully refreshing and a breeze to make in the food processor.

> 2 packages (10 ounces each) quick-thaw frozen strawberries
> 2 cartons (8 ounces each) plain yogurt
> ½ teaspoon finely grated orange or lemon rind

Partially thaw the strawberries (chunks of ice should still be visible in the packet), then dump into a food processor fitted with the metal chopping blade. Add yogurt and rind and buzz 60 seconds nonstop. Scrape work bowl sides down with a rubber spatula, then blend until creamy smooth with two 60-second churnings.

Dump into a 1½-pint freezer carton, snap on the lid and freeze several hours until mushy. Dump into processor (again fitted with the metal chopping blade) and buzz until creamy and light. Spoon back into carton, freeze until soft-firm and serve. Top, if you like, with a few fresh sliced strawberries. 125 calories per serving; add 25 calories for each ½ cup of unsweetened sliced strawberries.

Variations:

Frozen Raspberry Yogurt: Prepare as directed above, but substitute 2 packages (10 ounces each) quick-thaw frozen raspberries for the strawberries. 145 calories per serving.

Frozen Peach Yogurt: Dump 2 packages (10 ounces each) partially thawed frozen sliced peaches (the quick-thaw variety) into a food processor fitted with the metal chopping blade along with 2 cartons (8 ounces each) plain yogurt and a pinch each of ground ginger and nutmeg. Buzz until smooth, then freeze as directed. 132 calories per serving.

Frozen Raspberry-Strawberry Yogurt: Prepare as directed, but use 1 package (10 ounces) each quick-thaw frozen raspberries and strawberries. 135 calories per serving.

4
FRUITS AND FRUIT DESSERTS

BURGUNDY-POACHED PEARS WITH CRÈME ANGLAISE
Serves 6

A perfect pear dessert.

NOTE: The pears you use for this recipe should be firm-ripe and perfectly formed (Bosc, Bartlett, Anjou or Seckel are all good varieties to seek out). Choose an inexpensive jug wine for poaching the pears, then turn it into a bonus low-calorie dessert—Mulled Wine Jelly (see p. 87).

> 2 cups dry red wine (preferably a Burgundy type)
> 2 cups cold water
> 1 tablespoon lemon juice
> $\frac{1}{2}$ cinnamon stick
> 6 medium-size ripe pears
> 6 packets (1 gram each) aspartame sweetener

Sauce:

> 1 recipe Crème Anglaise (see p. 165)

In a large heavy saucepan (not aluminum, which might give the pears a metallic taste), combine the wine, water and lemon juice; drop in the cinnamon stick and set over low heat.

Using a swivel-bladed vegetable peeler or a fruit corer, core each whole pear by inserting the implement deep into the pear bottom, then twisting the core out as neatly as possible. Now peel each pear using the swivel-bladed peeler (for a prettier look, leave the stem on) and slide straight away into the wine mixture, stem-end up; baste with more of the mixture so that the pear doesn't darken. Once all pears are in the pan, adjust heat so that poaching liquid just trembles; cook the pears uncovered, basting often with poaching liquid, for 15 minutes. Remove from heat and cool pears to room temperature in the poaching liquid. Remove and discard the cinnamon stick. Now lift the pears from the kettle and set aside; stir the sweetener into the poaching liquid. Return the pears to the kettle, baste well with poaching liquid, cover and chill 1 to 2 hours, basting now and then.

Meanwhile, Prepare the Crème Anglaise As Directed: Cover and refrigerate until ready to serve.

To Serve: Lift the pears from the poaching liquid and stand stem-up in footed goblets. Spoon 4 tablespoons of Crème Anglaise over each pear and serve. 173 calories per serving.

SWEDISH CREAM WITH FRESH SLICED PEACHES

Serves 6

My original recipe for this cool, shimmering dessert calls for a full pint of heavy cream and another of sour cream, which boost the calorie count to a whopping 563 per serving—and that's *without* any fruit topping. This low-calorie version weighs in at just 212 calories per serving, *including* a generous ladling of fresh sliced peaches.

> 1 pint half-and-half cream
> 1 envelope plain gelatin
> ¾ cup evaporated skim milk
> 10 packets (1 gram each) aspartame sweetener
> 1½ cups plain yogurt
> 1½ teaspoons vanilla

Topping:

> 5 large ripe peaches, peeled and sliced thin
> 1 tablespoon lemon juice
> 3 packets (1 gram each) aspartame sweetener

Pour the half-and-half into a medium-size heavy saucepan, sprinkle the gelatin evenly over the surface and let soak for several minutes. Set over moderate heat and stir 3 to 4 minutes until gelatin dissolves completely. Off heat, stir in the evaporated skim milk and cool mixture to room temperature. Whisk in the sweetener, then the yogurt and vanilla. Cover and chill overnight until softly set.

Prepare the Topping Just Before Serving: Sprinkle the peaches with the lemon juice and toss well, then sprinkle with the sweetener and toss again. Layer the Swedish Cream and sliced peaches alternately into 6 goblets (I like to serve the dessert in the slender goblets I use for serving white wine), then sprig, if you wish, with lemon verbena or mint. 212 calories per serving.

Variations:

Swedish Cream with Fresh Strawberries: Prepare the Swedish Cream as directed; wash, hull and slice 1 pint fresh ripe strawberries, then sweeten to taste with aspartame sweetener (2 to 3 packets should be sufficient and you may need no sweetener at all). Layer into stemmed goblets and serve. 200 calories per serving.

Swedish Cream with Fresh Raspberries: Prepare the Swedish Cream as directed; wash 1 pint fresh ripe raspberries gently in cool water, then sweeten to taste with aspartame sweetener (2 to 3 packets should be sufficient and you may not need any sweetener). Layer into stemmed goblets and serve. 207 calories per serving.

ROTE GRÜTZE
Serves 12

This German favorite, filled with the red berries of summer (and smothered with heavy cream in the traditional recipe), is scarcely slimming. The original version, given to me by my Bavarian friend Hedy Wuerz, adds up to an astronomical 612 calories per serving. This pared-down version, however, is truly low calorie—a mere 160 per serving.

NOTE: This recipe makes a lot, it's true, but Rote Grütze keeps well in the refrigerator for about a week and, in fact, tastes even better after a day or two. It's best when topped by a little milk or cream and I give you a choice of toppings below ranging in calories from very low to moderate.

    1 package (10 ounces) quick-thaw frozen raspberries, thawed and drained (reserve juice)
    2 packages (10 ounces each) quick-thaw frozen strawberries, thawed and pureed
    3 cups cranberry juice cocktail
    2 teaspoons finely grated lemon rind
    ¼ cup lemon juice
    2 envelopes plain gelatin
    5 tablespoons cornstarch
    ½ cup dry red wine
  1½ pounds dark sweet cherries, stemmed, washed, pitted and quartered
  12 packages (1 gram each) aspartame sweetener

A Choice of Toppings:

Half-and-half cream (20 calories per tablespoon)
Mock Devonshire Cream (14 calories per tablespoon; see p. 179)
Whole milk (10 calories per tablespoon)
Plain yogurt (8 calories per tablespoon)
Buttermilk (6 calories per tablespoon)

Place the raspberry juice, pureed strawberries, cranberry juice cocktail, lemon rind and juice in a medium-size heavy saucepan (not aluminum, which might give the dessert a metallic taste); sprinkle the gelatin evenly over the surface and let stand a minute or two. Set over moderate heat and stir 3 to 4 minutes, just until gelatin dissolves. Quickly combine cornstarch and wine; whisk into the juice mixture, then cook and stir (keep below the boiling point) about 3 minutes, just until mixture thickens and clears. Add raspberries and cherries; cook and stir 1 minute.

Dump all into a large heatproof bowl and cool to room temperature; stir in the sweetener. Spoon into small dessert bowls or stemmed goblets and chill at least 12 hours before serving.

NOTE: Because Rote Grütze is softly rather than stiffly set, its surface will flatten on standing. For a prettier presentation, simply fork up the Rote Grütze lightly before serving or adding your choice of topping. 160 calories per serving exclusive of topping.

Serve as is or, if you prefer, trickle 2 to 3 tablespoons of one of the suggested toppings over each portion.

NOTE: The half-and-half is best but it's also the highest in calories, alas; second best, I think, is the Mock Devonshire Cream, 2 tablespoons of which ladled over a portion of Rote Grütze will increase the calorie count by only 28 calories, putting the grand total at a still-slimming 188 per serving.

DARK SWEET CHERRY COBBLER
Serves 8

Friends tell me this is the best cherry cobbler they've ever eaten—and yet there are fewer than 250 calories per serving (about a third less than what a good fudgy brownie contains). What makes it special, I think, is that the cherries used are fresh —the dark sweet cherries of summer. Don't substitute canned cherries for the fresh in this recipe or sour cherries for the sweet because you will be disappointed.

> 1½ cups cranberry juice cocktail
> ⅔ cup water
> 2 tablespoons plus 1 teaspoon quick-cooking tapioca
> 1¾ pounds fresh dark sweet cherries, stemmed, washed
>   and pitted
> ¼ teaspoon finely grated orange rind
> 1 teaspoon unsalted butter
> 4 packets (1 gram each) aspartame sweetener
> ½ teaspoon almond extract

Topping:

> 1½ cups unsifted self-rising flour
> ½ teaspoon finely grated orange rind
> 4 packets (1 gram each) aspartame sweetener
> ½ cup heavy cream
> 3 tablespoons evaporated milk

Place the cranberry juice cocktail, water and tapioca in a medium-size saucepan and allow to soak 15 minutes; set over moderately low heat and stir 4 to 5 minutes until thickened and clear. Dump in the cherries, cover, turn heat to the lowest point and simmer 10 minutes. Off the heat, stir in the orange rind and butter; cool to room temperature, stirring often to prevent a skin from forming on the surface of the sauce. Mix in the sweetener and almond extract and pour the cherry mixture into an ungreased 9″ x 9″ x 2″ baking dish. Set aside while you prepare the topping.

For the Topping: Combine the flour, orange rind and sweetener in a medium-size mixing bowl; combine the heavy cream and evaporated milk in a measuring cup. Make a well in the center of the dry ingredients, dump in the combined liquids all at once and fork briskly just until the dough clings together; if you overmix at this point, the topping will be tough.

Using a tablespoon, drop the dough in 9 mounds of equal size on top of the cherry mixture, spacing them evenly (there should be 3 rows of 3).

Bake the cobbler uncovered in a hot oven (400°F.) for 20 to 25 minutes or until the cherries bubble and the topping is touched with brown. Cool 30 minutes before serving. 247 calories per serving.

OLD-FASHIONED PEACH COBBLER
Serves 8

For this low-calorie dessert, I've taken an old family recipe and subtracted half the calories without sacrificing an ounce of flavor.

2 packages (1¼ pounds each) frozen unsweetened peach slices, partially thawed
¾ cup water
2 tablespoons quick-cooking tapioca
Juice of 1 lemon
¼ teaspoon ground cinnamon
¼ teaspoon ground mace
Pinch ground ginger
2 teaspoons unsalted butter
12 packets (1 gram each) aspartame sweetener
½ teaspoon vanilla
½ teaspoon almond extract

Topping:

1½ cups unsifted self-rising cake flour
1 teaspoon finely grated lemon rind
3 packets (1 gram each) aspartame sweetener
½ cup heavy cream
3 tablespoons evaporated milk

Drain the thawed peach juices into a small heavy saucepan; reserve the peaches. Add the water to the pan, sprinkle the tapioca evenly over the surface and allow to stand 5 minutes. Set over moderate heat and stir 4 to 5 minutes until the tapioca thickens and clears. Remove from the heat and stir in the lemon juice, cinnamon, mace, ginger and butter. Place the reserved peaches in a large heatproof bowl, pour in the tapioca mixture and stir to mix; cool to room temperature; mix in the sweetener, vanilla and almond extract. Pour all into an ungreased 9" x 9" x 2" baking dish and set aside while you prepare the topping.

For the Topping: In a medium-size mixing bowl, combine the flour, lemon rind and sweetener. In a measuring cup, combine the heavy cream and evaporated milk. Make a well in the center of the dry ingredients, then dump in the combined liquids. Stir briskly with a fork just until all dry ingredients are moistened and the mixture holds together. Do not overbeat at this point or the topping will be tough.

Using a tablespoon, drop the topping in 9 mounds of equal size on top of the peach mixture, spacing them evenly (you should have 3 rows of 3).

Bake uncovered in a hot oven (400°F.) for 20 to 25 minutes or until peaches are bubbly and topping is tipped with brown. Cool 30 minutes, then serve. 200 calories per serving.

STRAWBERRY SHORTCAKE
Serves 10

There are two camps when it comes to strawberry shortcake; those who like their shortcake to be a short biscuit (if you belong to that camp, I refer you to Drop Shortcakes; see p. 57) and those who like their shortcake to be a sponge cake (the recipe here is for you).

Shortcake:

$\frac{3}{4}$ cup unsifted cake flour
$\frac{1}{2}$ teaspoon baking powder
$\frac{1}{4}$ teaspoon salt
3 large eggs, separated
$\frac{1}{2}$ teaspoon vanilla
$\frac{2}{3}$ cup sugar
3 tablespoons water
$\frac{1}{2}$ teaspoon cream of tartar

Strawberries:

1 pint ripe strawberries, washed, hulled and sliced thin

Whipped Topping:

1 tablespoon water
1 teaspoon lemon juice
1 teaspoon plain gelatin
$\frac{1}{3}$ cup ice-cold evaporated milk
$\frac{1}{2}$ cup heavy cream
2 tablespoons confectioners' (10X) sugar
$\frac{1}{2}$ teaspoon vanilla

Garnish:

3 perfect strawberries

For the Shortcake: Line the bottom of an 8" layer-cake pan with wax paper; do not grease; set aside. Sift the flour with the baking powder and salt and set aside also. Beat the egg yolks and the vanilla until light and lemony. Gradually beat in the sugar. Now with the mixer set at low speed, add the dry ingredients alternately with the water, beginning and ending with the dry ingredients. Beat only enough to combine the ingredients, no longer, or you may toughen the shortcake. Beat the egg whites with the cream of tartar to stiff peaks; fold into the yolk mixture gently but thoroughly. Pour the batter into the prepared pan and bake in a moderately slow oven (325°F.) for 25 minutes or until a toothpick inserted in the center of the shortcake comes out clean. Turn the shortcake out at once on a cooling rack and peel off the wax paper. Cool completely.

With a sharp serrated knife, split the shortcake horizontally into two layers. Place one layer, cut-side up, on a serving plate; top with the sliced strawberries. Let stand while you prepare the topping.

For the Topping: Combine the water and lemon juice in a very small saucepan (a butter warmer is the perfect utensil); sprinkle the gelatin over the surface, set over low heat and stir just until the gelatin dissolves. Remove from the heat and cool. Beat the evaporated milk at highest mixer speed until it begins to thicken. Add the cooled gelatin mixture and continue beating until high peaks form; set aside. Beat the heavy cream until it begins to thicken. Add the 10X sugar and vanilla and continue beating until stiff peaks form. Fold the whipped mixtures together.

Spread 1 cup of the topping over the strawberries, top with the remaining shortcake layer, placing it cut-side down. Spread the remaining whipped topping on top of the shortcake and garnish by placing a cluster of perfect strawberries in the center.

NOTE: This shortcake tastes best if eaten within about 3 hours; if you wait longer, the topping will begin to break down. 175 calories per serving.

FRESH APPLE-PECAN TORTE
Serves 8

A variation on everyone's favorite—date-nut pudding—that's significantly slimmed down.

1 large egg
⅓ cup firmly packed light brown sugar
⅓ cup granulated sugar
¼ teaspoon finely grated orange rind
½ cup unsifted self-rising cake flour
2 large tart green apples, peeled, cored and chopped
    fine (you should have 1⅓ cups chopped apple)
½ teaspoon vanilla
⅓ cup chopped pecans

Topping:

1 recipe Low-Calorie Whipped "Cream" (see p. 178)

Beat the egg with the light brown and granulated sugars and orange rind until thick and lemony. Add the flour alternately with the chopped apples, beginning and ending with the flour and mixing only enough after each addition to moisten the dry ingredients. Stir in the vanilla and pecans.

Spoon into a 9″ pie pan that has been sprayed with nonstick vegetable cooking spray and bake in a moderate oven (350°F.) for about 30 minutes until soft-firm to the touch and the torte begins to pull from the sides of the pan.

Remove from the oven and cool upright in the pan on a wire rack for 30 minutes. Cut into 8 wedges and serve topped by a spoonful or two of Low-Calorie Whipped "Cream." 145 calories per serving. Add 3 calories for each tablespoon of Low-Calorie Whipped "Cream" used.

GRANDMA'S APPLE BROWN BETTY
Serves 6

Everything about this Apple Brown Betty is just like my Grandmother Johnson's—except the calories, which I've cut in half. The best apples to use? Tart, *authoritative* ones—Greenings, Macs, Rome Beauties, etc.

> 4 slices stale firm-textured white bread
> 1 tablespoon unsalted butter, at room temperature
> 2 tablespoons light brown sugar
> 6 packets (1 gram each) aspartame sweetener
> $\frac{1}{2}$ teaspoon ground cinnamon
> $\frac{1}{4}$ teaspoon ground nutmeg
> Rind of 1 lemon, grated fine
> Juice of $\frac{1}{2}$ lemon
> 1 cup unsweetened applesauce
> 5 largish tart apples, peeled, cored and sliced thin
> $\frac{1}{3}$ cup water

Butter 3 slices of the bread on one side, stack them and cut into $\frac{1}{2}''$ cubes; buzz the remaining slice of bread to coarse crumbs; set both aside.

Combine the brown sugar, sweetener, cinnamon, nutmeg and lemon rind, pressing out any lumps. Mix in the lemon juice and applesauce, dump in the apples and reserved bread cubes and toss lightly to mix. Spoon into a shallow 6-cup casserole that has been lightly sprayed with nonstick vegetable cooking spray, pour in the water, cover snugly with foil and bake in a hot oven (400°F.) for 40 to 45 minutes or until the apples are juicy and firm-tender. Discard the foil cover, scatter the reserved crumbs evenly on top and bake 15 minutes longer in the 400°F. oven or until bubbling and touched with brown. Serve warm, topped, if you like, by a little whole milk. 148 calories per serving. Add 10 calories for each tablespoon of milk used.

DOWN EAST BLUEBERRY BREAD PUDDING
Serves 6

I urge you to make the most of the fresh blueberry season by serving this surprisingly rich, low-calorie pudding. It's best warm, topped with a little milk.

2 tablespoons sugar
1 tablespoon cornstarch
10 packets (1 gram each) aspartame sweetener
½ teaspoon finely grated orange rind
1 pint fresh blueberries, washed, sorted and stemmed
    Juice of ½ large lemon
4 slices stale firm-textured white bread
1 tablespoon unsalted butter, at room temperature
½ cup evaporated skim milk

Combine the sugar, cornstarch, sweetener and orange rind, pressing out all lumps. Dump the blueberries into a 6-cup shallow casserole that has been lightly sprayed with nonstick vegetable cooking spray. Dump in the sugar mixture, add the lemon juice and toss well to mix. With a potato masher, lightly mash the blueberries; set aside. Butter 3 slices of the bread lightly on one side, stack the slices and cut into ½" cubes. Dump into the casserole and toss well to mix. Buzz the remaining slice of bread to coarse crumbs and reserve. Bake the pudding uncovered in a moderate oven (350°F.) for 30 minutes; remove from the oven, add the evaporated skim milk and stir well to mix. Sprinkle the reserved crumbs evenly on top, return to the moderate oven and bake uncovered for 15 minutes. Serve warm, topped, if you like, by a little whole milk. 132 calories per serving; add 10 calories for each tablespoon of milk used.

BLUEBERRIES IN SNOW
Serves 4

Once you've washed, sorted and stemmed the blueberries, you've virtually made the dessert: The "snow" can be stirred up in no time flat.

    1 pint fresh blueberries
    6 packets (1 gram each) aspartame sweetener
    $\frac{2}{3}$ cup plain yogurt
    $\frac{1}{3}$ cup sour cream
    $\frac{1}{8}$ teaspoon finely grated orange rind
    $\frac{1}{2}$ teaspoon vanilla
    $\frac{1}{8}$ teaspoon almond extract

Wash the berries under cool running water, rejecting any that are shriveled or green; remove stems, then pat the berries very dry between several thicknesses of paper toweling.

NOTE: It's imperative that the berries be very dry; otherwise they will water down the sauce. Place the berries in a small mixing bowl, sprinkle 4 packets of the sweetener evenly over all and toss to mix; set aside.

In a small bowl, combine the yogurt, sour cream, remaining 2 packets of sweetener, orange rind, vanilla and almond extract.

To serve, spoon the berries into 4 bowl-shaped wine goblets, then drift the snowy sauce lightly on top of each portion. 110 calories per serving.

GREEN GRAPES IN YOGURT SAUCE WITH MANGO
Serves 6

I always feel virtuous when I eat this dessert because it's low in calories and high in vitamins A and C. It's also delicious.

- 1½ cups seedless green grapes, washed, patted very dry on paper toweling and chilled several hours in the refrigerator
- 1½ cups of ½" cubes of ripe mango, chilled several hours in the refrigerator
- 1 cup plain yogurt
- ½ cup sour cream
- 3 packets (1 gram each) aspartame sweetener
- ¼ teaspoon finely grated orange rind
- ½ teaspoon vanilla
- ⅛ teaspoon almond extract
- 2 tablespoons raw sugar

Place the grapes and mango in a medium-size mixing bowl and toss lightly to mix; set aside. Combine the yogurt, sour cream, sweetener, orange rind, vanilla and almond extract, pour over the fruit mixture and toss lightly. Spoon into dessert dishes or stemmed goblets and sprinkle each portion lightly with raw sugar. 126 calories per serving.

PINEAPPLE FANS WITH COINTREAU AND CRÈME DE MENTHE

Serves 6

This is the accommodating sort of dessert that can be made well ahead of time, then kept in the refrigerator until you are ready to serve it—in fact, it profits from a stay in the fridge. I prefer to use white *crème de menthe* for macerating the pineapple, but the green can be used equally well; it will tint the pineapple fans a pale spring green.

> 1 medium-size ripe pineapple (2½ to 3 pounds)
> 1 tablespoon white or green *crème de menthe*
> 1 tablespoon Cointreau

Slice off the stem and butt ends of the pineapple, then stand the pineapple on a cutting board, and with a very sharp knife, slice straight down removing the prickly peeling. Continue slicing straight down the pineapple until all skin is removed, trying to cut just deep enough to get out all prickly brown bits. Quarter the pineapple vertically, then halve each quarter lengthwise so that you have 8 long wedges. Slice the point (core) off each wedge, then slice each wedge about ⅛″ thick; place all in a large mixing bowl, add the *crème de menthe* and Cointreau and toss lightly to mix. Cover and macerate several hours in the refrigerator. Toss well again, spoon into stemmed goblets and sprig with mint. 63 calories per serving.

AMBROSIA
Serves 6

An Olympian dessert brought down to earth. Make this several hours ahead of time and allow to macerate (steep) in the refrigerator so that the flavors have a chance to mellow and mingle.

3 large navel oranges
1 small very ripe pineapple
3 packets (1 gram each) aspartame sweetener
½ cup freshly grated coconut
2 tablespoons Cointreau

Peel the oranges, making sure that you remove all of the bitter, white inner skin; halve the oranges from navel end to butt end and slice each half about ¼" thick. Place in a nonmetallic bowl. Slice the top and bottom ends off the pineapple, stand the pineapple on a cutting board, and with a very sharp knife, make a series of cuts straight down, removing all of the prickly peeling. Quarter the pineapple vertically, halve each quarter lengthwise and slice the point (core) off of each wedge. Slice each piece of pineapple very thin; place in a nonmetallic bowl.

To assemble the Ambrosia, alternate layers of pineapple and orange slices in a pretty crystal bowl, sprinkling as you go with sweetener and coconut. Drizzle in any orange or pineapple juice remaining in the bowls, then the Cointreau, cover and chill several hours. 91 calories per serving.

5

CAKES AND COOKIES, FILLINGS AND FROSTINGS

ANGEL FOOD CAKE
Serves 12 to 14

Angel food cakes, bless them, are largely air, meaning they are very low in calories. They are also uncommonly versatile, perfectly delicious when topped with fresh sliced peaches or strawberries, when sauced with Crème Anglaise, Zabaglione or Melba Sauce. And, of course, they're delicious eaten out of hand.

NOTE: Always use a serrated knife when slicing angel food cake. Begin by standing the knife on its point in the central hole; then, using a gentle up-and-down sawing motion, slice through the cake, keeping the knife blade perpendicular the whole time. This way you are exerting no pressure at all on the top of the cake and thus will not compact it.

    1 cup unsifted cake flour
    1⅓ cups superfine sugar
    12 large egg whites
    ½ teaspoon cream of tartar
    1 teaspoon vanilla
    ¼ teaspoon almond extract

Sift the flour with ⅔ cup of the sugar onto a piece of wax paper and set aside. Beat the egg whites with the cream of tartar until soft and billowing. Beat in the remaining ⅔ cup of sugar, 2 tablespoons at a time; continue beating until the whites are stiff but not dry. Fold in the vanilla and almond extract. Sift the sugar-flour mixture, about half of the total amount at a time, over the egg whites and fold in gently but completely. Spoon the batter into an ungreased 10″ tube pan, run a spatula gently through the batter in the pan to deflate any air pockets. Bake in a moderate oven (350°F.) for 40 to 45 minutes or until pale tan and springy to the touch. Remove the cake from the oven, invert at once and let the cake cool in the upside-down pan for 1 hour. When cool, loosen the cake around the edges and around the central tube with a thin-blade spatula, then turn out. 134 calories for each of 12 servings, 115 for each of 14.

CLASSIC SPONGE CAKE
Serves 12

Spoon sliced ripe strawberries or peaches over wedges of this feathery sponge cake, top with any fruit sauce or enjoy eating as is.

 6 large eggs, at room temperature
 1 cup sifted superfine sugar
 $\frac{1}{4}$ teaspoon salt
 $\frac{1}{4}$ teaspoon finely grated lemon rind
 1 teaspoon lemon juice
 1 teaspoon vanilla
 1 cup sifted all-purpose flour

Separate the eggs, placing the whites in a large mixing bowl and the yolks in a second large mixing bowl. Beat the yolks until thick, add the sugar gradually, beating all the while, then beat in the salt, lemon rind, lemon juice and vanilla. Continue beating until the eggs are the color and consistency of mayonnaise. Add the flour gradually, beating at lowest mixer speed. Now beat the egg whites to soft peaks; mix about $\frac{1}{2}$ cup of the beaten whites into the batter, then gently but thoroughly fold in the remaining beaten whites until no streaks of white or yellow remain.

Pour the batter into an ungreased 10″ tube pan and bake in a moderate oven (350°F.) for 45 to 50 minutes or until lightly browned and springy to the touch. Remove the cake from the oven, invert at once and cool 1 hour in the upside-down pan. Turn the cooled cake right-side up, loosen around the edges and around the central tube with a thin-blade spatula and turn out onto a cake plate. With a sharp serrated knife, cut into 12 wedges and serve. 133 calories per serving.

CELESTIAL MARBLE CAKE
Serves 12 to 14

Why celestial? This marble cake, unlike the conventional butter-rich ones, is composed of two angel cake batters, one vanilla, one chocolate.

Chocolate Batter:

6 tablespoons cake flour
2 tablespoons cocoa powder (not a mix)
$\frac{2}{3}$ cup superfine sugar
6 large egg whites
$\frac{1}{4}$ teaspoon cream of tartar
$\frac{1}{2}$ teaspoon vanilla

Vanilla Batter:

$\frac{1}{2}$ cup unsifted cake flour
$\frac{2}{3}$ cup superfine sugar
6 large egg whites
$\frac{1}{4}$ teaspoon cream of tartar
$\frac{1}{2}$ teaspoon vanilla extract
$\frac{1}{4}$ teaspoon almond extract

For the Chocolate Batter: Sift the flour and cocoa together three times, then sift again with $\frac{1}{3}$ cup of the sugar; set aside. Beat the egg whites with the cream of tartar until soft and billowing. Add the remaining $\frac{1}{3}$ cup sugar, 1 tablespoon at a time; continue beating until stiff but not dry. Fold in the vanilla. Sift the sugar-flour mixture over the beaten whites and fold in thoroughly using a gentle touch; set aside.

For the Vanilla Batter: Sift the flour with $\frac{1}{3}$ cup of the sugar and set aside. Beat the egg whites and the cream of tartar until soft and billowing. Add the remaining $\frac{1}{3}$ cup sugar, 1 tablespoon at a time, and continue beating until stiff and glossy. Fold in the vanilla and almond extract. Sift the sugar-flour mixture over the

135

beaten whites and fold in gently but completely.

Now spoon the batters into an ungreased 10″ tube pan, alternating the flavors, i.e., one spoonful of chocolate, one spoonful of vanilla, one spoonful of chocolate and so on. To create a marbled effect, cut through the batter in four places using a thin-blade spatula.

Bake the cake in a moderate oven (350°F.) for 40 to 45 minutes or until the cake begins to pull from the sides of the pan and is firm to the touch. Remove the cake from the oven, invert at once and cool in the upside-down pan for 1 hour. Loosen the cake around the edges and around the central tube with a thin-blade spatula, then turn out.

NOTE: Use the same technique for cutting this cake as you would for angel food cake, that is, use a sharp serrated knife and a gentle sawing motion so that you don't deflate or compact the cake. 135 calories for each of 12 servings, 115 calories for each of 14.

FRESH ORANGE CAKE
Serves 8

This cake is so good you'd never dream that it's a low-calorie dessert.

Cake:

$\frac{3}{4}$ cup unsifted cake flour
$\frac{1}{2}$ teaspoon baking powder
$\frac{1}{4}$ teaspoon salt
3 large eggs, separated
$\frac{2}{3}$ cup sugar
3 tablespoons fresh orange juice
1 teaspoon finely grated orange rind
$\frac{1}{2}$ teaspoon cream of tartar

Orange Pastry Cream Filling:

2 tablespoons sugar
2 tablespoons cornstarch
1 large egg yolk, lightly beaten
$\frac{3}{4}$ cup skim milk
Pinch of salt
$\frac{1}{2}$ cup orange juice
1 teaspoon vanilla
2 teaspoons plain gelatin
$\frac{1}{2}$ cup ice-cold evaporated skim milk

Decoration:

$\frac{1}{2}$ navel orange, sliced thin

For the Cake: Sift the flour with the baking powder and salt onto a piece of wax paper; set aside. Beat the egg yolks hard until light and lemon colored; add the sugar gradually, beating all the while, then continue beating until mixture is the color and consistency of mayonnaise. Combine the orange juice and rind. Now, with mixer set at low speed, add to the yolk mixture the dry ingredients alternately with the orange juice, beginning and ending with the dry ingredients and beating after each addition just enough to combine. Beat the egg whites with the cream of tartar until stiff, then fold gently but thoroughly into the cake batter.

Pour batter into an 8″ layer-cake pan that has been lined with wax paper. Bake in a moderately slow oven (325°F.) for 25 minutes or until a toothpick inserted in the center of the cake comes out clean. Remove the cake from the oven, loosen around the edges with a thin-blade spatula, then invert on a cake rack and peel off the wax paper. Cool the cake to room temperature.

Meanwhile, Prepare the Orange Pastry Cream Filling: In a small saucepan, combine the sugar and cornstarch, pressing out any lumps. Now combine the egg yolk and milk, pour into pan and stir to combine. Set over moderate heat and cook, stirring constantly, 3 to 4 minutes, just until thickened and clear and no raw starch taste lingers. Off heat, stir in salt, ¼ cup of the orange juice and the vanilla. Cool to room temperature, whisking often to prevent a skin from forming on the surface of the sauce, then cover loosely and chill until slightly thickened.

Combine the remaining ¼ cup of orange juice with the gelatin in a very small heavy saucepan or butter warmer (*not* unlined copper), set over moderate heat and stir 3 to 4 minutes until gelatin dissolves completely; cool to room temperature. Beat evaporated skim milk at high mixer speed until it begins to thicken; add the orange-gelatin mixture and continue beating until mixture forms stiff peaks. Gently fold this whipped mixture into the chilled pastry cream.

To Assemble the Cake: Halve the cake horizontally and place one layer cut-side up on a cake plate. Spread with 1 cup of the pastry cream. Top with remaining layer, cut-side down, then spread remaining pastry cream on the top and sides of the cake. To decorate the cake, halve the orange slices, then stand them on top of the cake, radiating out from the center like spokes of a wheel.

Keep the cake refrigerated until ready to serve. 185 calories for each of 8 pieces.

BLACK FOREST CAKE
Serves 10 to 12

This is a very pretty cake because the cherries and cream sandwiched in between the chocolate layers are clearly visible. And would you believe 153 calories per serving?

Cake:

$\frac{1}{2}$ cup unsifted cake flour

3 tablespoons cocoa powder (not a mix)

$\frac{7}{8}$ cup sugar

8 large egg whites, at room temperature

$\frac{1}{2}$ teaspoon cream of tartar

1 teaspoon vanilla

Filling:

2 tablespoons Kirsch

1 teaspoon plain gelatin

1 can (16 ounces) water-packed, pitted sour red cherries, drained (reserve juice)

2 tablespoons granulated sugar

1 tablespoon cornstarch

$\frac{1}{2}$ cup cherry juice (drained from the can of cherries)

$\frac{1}{3}$ cup heavy cream

2 tablespoons confectioners' (10X) sugar

$\frac{1}{2}$ teaspoon vanilla extract

$\frac{1}{3}$ cup ice-cold evaporated milk

1 teaspoon lemon juice

For the Cake: Sift the flour and cocoa together three times, then sift again with $\frac{1}{2}$ cup of the sugar and set aside. Beat the egg whites with the cream of tartar to soft peaks. Add the remaining sugar, a tablespoon at a time, and continue beating until glossy and stiff. Fold in the vanilla. Using two to three installments, sift the flour mixture over the beaten whites and fold in gently but thoroughly. Divide the batter between two 8″ layer-cake pans that have been lined with wax paper but not greased. Smooth the surface of the batter in each pan, then bake in a moderately hot oven (375°F.) for 20 to 25 minutes or until layers are springy to the touch. Remove cakes from oven, invert at once on wire racks and cool upside down in the pan. When completely cool, loosen each cake layer around the edges with a thin-blade spatula, turn out and peel off the wax paper. Set the layers aside while you prepare the filling.

For the Filling: Place the Kirsch in a very small, heavy saucepan; sprinkle the gelatin on top and let stand 5 minutes. Set over very low heat and stir until gelatin dissolves; work carefully because the Kirsch is flammable. Remove from the heat and set aside to cool. Dump the cherries into a heatproof bowl and reserve also.

In a small saucepan, combine the sugar and cornstarch, pressing out all lumps, then mix in the cherry juice. Bring to a boil over moderate heat, stirring all the while, then let mixture bubble 1 minute longer until it thickens and clears. Mix into the cherries and reserve.

In a small bowl, beat the heavy cream to soft peaks. Add the 10X sugar and vanilla. Continue beating until very stiff. In smallest mixer bowl, combine the evaporated milk and lemon juice. Beat at high speed until very stiff. Beat in the cooled Kirsch-gelatin mixture. Finally, fold the whipped cream into the whipped evaporated milk.

To Assemble the Black Forest Cake: Place one cake layer on a small cake plate. Spread with the cherry mixture, pushing it right to the edge. Carefully spread 1 cup of the whipped cream mixture over the cherries, again, right to the edge. Top with the second layer. Fit a pastry bag with a star tip and fill with the remaining whipped cream mixture. Pipe rosettes around the top of the cake. Pipe any additional cream in a design in the center. Chill the cake until serving time. Cut into wedges and serve. 184 calories for each of 10 servings, 153 calories for each of 12 servings.

BOSTON CREAM PIE
Serves 8 to 10

You would never suspect that this is a low-calorie dessert. It's *that* good.

Cake:

3/4 cup unsifted cake flour
1/2 teaspoon baking powder
1/4 teaspoon salt
3 large eggs, separated
1/2 teaspoon vanilla
2/3 cup sugar
3 tablespoons water
1/2 teaspoon cream of tartar

Filling:

1 cup skim milk
2 tablespoons cornstarch
1 large egg yolk
1 teaspoon vanilla
Pinch salt
3 packets (1 gram each) aspartame sweetener

Chocolate Frosting:

1/2 cup unsifted confectioners' (10X) sugar
2 tablespoons cocoa powder (not a mix)
1 tablespoon very hot water
1 teaspoon unsalted butter, at room temperature

For the Cake: Line the bottom of an 8" layer-cake pan with wax paper; do not grease; set aside. Sift the flour with the baking powder and salt and set aside also. Beat the egg yolks and the vanilla until light and lemon colored. Gradually beat in the sugar. Now with the mixer set at low speed, add the dry ingredients alternately with the water, beginning and ending with the dry ingredients. Beat only enough to combine the ingredients, no longer or you will toughen the cake. Beat the egg whites with the cream of tartar to stiff peaks; fold into the yolk mixture gently but thoroughly. Pour the batter into the prepared pan and bake in a moderately slow oven (325°F.) for 25 minutes or until a toothpick inserted in the center of the cake comes out clean. Turn the cake out at once on a cooling rack and peel off the wax paper. Cool to room temperature.

Meanwhile, Prepare the Filling: In a small heavy saucepan, combine the milk and cornstarch, whisking until completely homogeneous. Set over moderate heat and stir 3 to 4 minutes until the mixture bubbles up, thickens and clears. Whisk about $\frac{1}{4}$ cup of the hot mixture into the egg yolk, stir back into saucepan and heat and stir about 1 minute. Off heat, mix in the vanilla and salt. Cool to room temperature, whisking now and then to prevent a skin from forming on the surface of the sauce; blend in the sweetener.

For the Frosting: Stir together the 10X sugar and cocoa, pressing out all lumps. Add the water and stir until smooth; blend in the butter.

To Assemble the Cream Pie: With a sharp serrated knife, split the cake horizontally into two layers. Place one layer, cut-side up, on a serving plate. Spread with the cooled filling. Top with the second layer, placing it cut-side down. Frost the top layer, letting a little of the chocolate frosting dribble down the sides of the cake.

NOTE: If the frosting is too thick to spread easily, thin with a few drops of hot water. 200 calories for each of 8 servings, 160 calories for each of 10.

CAUTION: Since this cake contains an egg-rich cream filling, store any leftovers in the refrigerator. If you leave it at room temperature, you are flirting with food poisoning.

CHOCOLATE-ORANGE-PECAN TORTE

Serves 16

This high-rising, European-style tube cake contains no flour at all, only fine bread and cookie crumbs, which together with stiffly beaten egg whites, account for the spongy texture. Serve the torte as is, or if you like, split into three layers and sandwich together with Tart Orange Filling. You'll increase the calorie count only slightly.

> 12 old-fashioned thin chocolate wafers (those measuring $2\frac{1}{4}''$ in diameter), buzzed to fine crumbs (you should have $\frac{3}{4}$ cup crumbs)
> 2 slices firm-textured white bread, buzzed to fine crumbs (1 cup crumbs)
> $\frac{1}{2}$ cup pecan meats, ground very fine (they should be feathery; if you have a food processor, so much the better because it will buzz the nuts to perfection)
> Rind of $\frac{1}{2}$ orange, grated fine
> $1\frac{1}{2}$ cups superfine sugar
> 8 large egg yolks
> 1 teaspoon vanilla
> $\frac{1}{2}$ teaspoon almond extract
> 10 large egg whites
> $\frac{1}{8}$ teaspoon salt

Filling (Optional):

> 1 recipe Tart Orange Filling, prepared as directed (see p. 159)

Line the bottom of a 10″ tube pan (preferably one with a removable bottom) with wax paper; do not grease the paper and do not grease the pan. Set aside while you prepare the cake.

Place the cookie crumbs, bread crumbs, nuts and rind in a large mixing bowl; toss well to mix; set aside. Beat $\frac{3}{4}$ cup of the

144

sugar with the egg yolks until the color and consistency of mayonnaise; add the vanilla and almond extract and beat hard; dump on top of the crumbs and stir well to mix.

Place the egg whites in a very large bowl, sprinkle in the salt, then beat until frothy. Add 2 tablespoons of the remaining sugar and beat until silvery. Add another 2 tablespoons of sugar and beat until mixture begins to thicken. Continue adding the rest of the sugar gradually, beating all the while, until the egg whites form stiff peaks.

Mix about one-fourth of the beaten whites into the yolk mixture (this is to lighten it and facilitate folding in the balance of the beaten whites). Now dump the remaining whites on top of the yolk mixture and fold in gently but thoroughly until no streaks of white or brown remain.

Pour the batter into the prepared pan and bake in a moderate oven (350°F.) for 1 to $1\frac{1}{4}$ hours or until the cake nearly fills the pan, is nicely browned and springy to the touch (it will also smell irresistible). Remove the cake from the oven and invert at once; cool the cake in the upside-down pan for 1 hour.

Turn the cake right-side up, loosen around the edges and around the central tube with a thin-blade spatula and turn out. Very carefully peel off the wax paper, unsticking any recalcitrant areas by dampening the paper lightly. Turn the cake upside down again and cool for another hour before cutting or filling.

NOTE: The cake will fall somewhat on cooling but that is as it should be.

To Fill the Cake: Split the cake horizontally into three layers of equal size (the easiest way to do this is to mark the layers off first with toothpicks, then to cut gradually around the cake using a sharp serrated knife and a gentle sawing motion; next, deepen the initial cuts until you have separated the cake into layers).

Now sandwich the cake together with the Tart Orange Filling, using plenty of it and keeping the layers in proper order. You can glaze the top of the cake with a little of the filling, if you like, but do not spread any on the sides of the cake; it will look messy. Let the filled cake stand at room temperature for at least one hour before cutting (if the day is very hot, let the cake stand in the refrigerator).

To serve, cut into 16 wedges using a sharp serrated knife and a gentle sawing motion. 162 calories per serving for the unfilled cake, 188 per serving for the filled cake.

APRICOT-ALMOND ROLL
Serves 8

The sort of dessert dieters dream of, but this one, praised be, can be enjoyed without sabotaging the day's calorie quota.

Cake:

$\frac{2}{3}$ cup sugar
$\frac{1}{2}$ cup unsifted cake flour
$\frac{3}{4}$ cup egg whites (about 5 to 6 large eggs)
$\frac{3}{4}$ teaspoon cream of tartar
$\frac{1}{4}$ teaspoon salt
$\frac{1}{2}$ teaspoon almond extract
$\frac{1}{2}$ teaspoon vanilla
2 tablespoons confectioners' (10X) sugar

Apricot Filling:

2 cans (16 ounces each) unsweetened, water-packed apricot halves, drained well
1 tablespoon sugar
$\frac{1}{2}$ teaspoon almond extract

Topping:

$\frac{1}{3}$ cup heavy cream, whipped to soft peaks
2 tablespoons toasted sliced almonds

For the Cake: Sift together $\frac{1}{3}$ cup of the sugar and all of the flour; set aside. Beat the egg whites with the cream of tartar and salt until soft peaks form. Add the remaining $\frac{1}{3}$ cup sugar, 1 tablespoon at a time, and beat until stiff but not dry. Fold in the almond extract and vanilla. In two to three installments, sift the flour mixture over the egg whites and fold in gently but completely. Spread the batter evenly in a foil-lined $15\frac{1}{2}''$ x $10\frac{1}{2}''$ x $1''$ jelly-roll pan. Bake 12 to 15 minutes in a moderately hot oven

(375°F.) until springy to the touch and lightly browned.

Meanwhile, set a large wire rack on the counter, spread a tea towel on top and sprinkle lightly with the 10X sugar. As soon as the cake is done, loosen around the edges with a thin-blade spatula, invert at once on the tea towel, and peel off the foil. Do not roll the cake up in the towel; just let it cool.

For the Filling: Puree the apricots in a food processor fitted with the metal chopping blade, in an electric blender at high speed or by forcing through a food mill. Dump the puree into a small heavy saucepan, stir in the sugar, set over moderate heat and cook and stir about 10 minutes, just until mixture begins to thicken. Off heat, stir in the almond extract; cool.

To Assemble the Roll: Spread the cake with the filling, leaving $\frac{1}{2}$" margins all around. Roll the cake up the short way so that you have a roll $10\frac{1}{2}$" long. Let stand at room temperature an hour or two.

To Serve: Ease the roll onto a small platter, spread with whipped cream and sprinkle with toasted almond slices. Slice—slightly on the diagonal—into 8 generous pieces. 210 calories per serving.

CHOCOLATE ROULADE WITH CHEESE AND CHOCOLATE FILLING
Serves 8

A lot more slimming than it looks or tastes.

Cake:

  6 tablespoons cake flour
  2 tablespoons cocoa powder (not a mix)
  ⅔ cup sugar
  6 large egg whites
  ¼ teaspoon cream of tartar
  ½ teaspoon vanilla
  2 tablespoons confectioners' (10X) sugar

Cheese and Chocolate Filling:

  1 pound low-fat ricotta cheese, drained very dry
  3 tablespoons sugar
  1 square (1 ounce) semisweet chocolate, chopped fine
  1 tablespoon chopped toasted blanched almonds
  1½ teaspoons finely grated orange rind

Topping:

  1 tablespoon sifted confectioners' (10X) sugar

For the Cake: Sift the flour with the cocoa three times, then sift with ⅓ cup of the sugar and set aside. Beat the egg whites with the cream of tartar until soft peaks form. Add the remaining ⅓ cup sugar, a tablespoon at a time, then continue beating until the meringue is stiff but not dry. Fold in the vanilla. Using two to three installments, sift the dry ingredients over the meringue and fold in gently but thoroughly. Spread the batter in a foil-lined 15½″ x 10½″ x 1″ jelly-roll pan. Bake in a moderately hot oven (375°F.) for 12 to 15 minutes or until cake is springy to the touch.

Meanwhile, spread a tea towel on a large wire rack and sprinkle evenly with the 10X sugar. As soon as the cake is done, loosen around the edges with a thin-blade spatula, invert at once on the tea towel and peel off the foil. Do not roll the cake up in the towel, but do let it cool.

For the Filling: In a food processor fitted with the metal chopping blade or in an electric mixer set at high speed, cream the ricotta and sugar hard for 2 minutes. Stir in remaining ingredients.

To Assemble the Roll: Spread the cake with the filling, leaving $\frac{1}{2}''$ margins all around. Roll the cake up the short way so that you have a roll $10\frac{1}{2}''$ long. Cover and refrigerate several hours to allow the flavors to mingle.

To Serve: Ease the roll onto a decorative small platter, sift the 10X sugar lightly over the top, then slice—slightly on the bias—into 8 generous pieces. 200 calories per serving.

LADYFINGERS
Makes 2 Dozen

These can be eaten as is or used as the foundation of such lavish desserts as Strawberry Chiffon Charlotte (see p. 194).

$\frac{1}{4}$ cup unsifted cake flour
$\frac{1}{3}$ cup confectioners' (10X) sugar
2 eggs, separated
$\frac{1}{4}$ teaspoon vanilla
$\frac{1}{8}$ teaspoon salt

Topping:

1 tablespoon sifted confectioners' (10X) sugar

Sift the flour with 3 tablespoons of the 10X sugar and set aside. Beat the egg yolks and vanilla hard until the color and consistency of mayonnaise. Beat the egg whites to soft peaks, add the remaining 10X sugar and the salt and beat until stiff and glossy. Gently fold the egg yolk mixture into the whites, then sprinkle the flour mixture on top and fold in using as light a touch as possible.

Fill a pastry tube fitted with a plain $\frac{1}{2}''$ tip with batter, then press out onto a foil-lined baking sheet (the shiny side of the foil should be down) into strips about 2" x $\frac{3}{4}''$. Bake in a moderate oven (350°F.) for 12 to 15 minutes until golden brown and springy to the touch.

Remove the Ladyfingers from the oven, then lift from the foil with a spatula and cool on wire racks. Top with a light dusting of 10X sugar. 10 calories per Ladyfinger.

MELTING MOMENTS
Makes 6 Dozen

A delicate, crisp Scottish cookie.

$\frac{1}{2}$ cup (1 stick) unsalted butter
1 cup unsifted confectioners' (10X) sugar
2 packets (1 gram each) aspartame sweetener
   Rind of 1$\frac{1}{2}$ large lemons, grated fine
1 teaspoon vanilla
2 large eggs
1$\frac{1}{2}$ cups sifted cornstarch

Cream the butter, 10X sugar, sweetener, lemon rind and vanilla until fluffy light. Beat in the eggs, then stir in the cornstarch.

Spray baking sheets lightly with nonstick vegetable cooking spray (if you spray the sheets too heavily, the cookies will run all over the sheet). Using the $\frac{1}{2}$ teaspoon measure of a measuring spoon set, scoop up lightly rounded spoonfuls of dough and drop onto the baking sheets, spacing 2$\frac{1}{2}$" apart (these cookies spread considerably as they bake).

Bake in a moderately hot oven (375°F.) 6 to 8 minutes or until ringed with tan. Transfer at once to wire racks to cool. Store airtight to keep the cookies crisp. 20 calories per cookie.

BROWN-EDGE ORANGE WAFERS
Makes 6 Dozen

These cookies suffer in humid weather, so choose a dry sunny day for making them and store them in an airtight cannister to keep them crisp.

$\frac{1}{2}$ cup (1 stick) unsalted butter
1 cup unsifted confectioners' (10X) sugar
2 packets (1 gram each) aspartame sweetener
   Rind of 1 large orange, grated fine
$\frac{1}{2}$ teaspoon vanilla
$\frac{1}{4}$ teaspoon almond extract
$\frac{1}{4}$ teaspoon ground mace
2 large eggs
1$\frac{1}{2}$ cups sifted cornstarch

Cream the butter, 10X sugar, sweetener, orange rind, vanilla, almond extract and mace until fluffy light. Beat in the eggs, then mix in the cornstarch.

Spray baking sheets lightly with nonstick vegetable cooking spray (if you spray the sheets too heavily, the cookies will run together). Using the $\frac{1}{2}$ teaspoon measure of a measuring spoon set, scoop up lightly rounded spoonfuls of dough and drop onto the baking sheets, spacing 2$\frac{1}{2}$″ apart (these cookies spread considerably as they bake).

Bake in a moderately hot oven (375°F.) 6 to 8 minutes or until ringed with tan. Transfer at once to wire racks to cool. 20 calories per cookie.

BUTTERMILK–WHEAT GERM CRISPS
Makes 5 Dozen

Only 29 calories apiece, these crisp cookies are the perfect accompaniment to a fresh fruit dessert. To *keep* them crisp, store in an airtight cannister.

$\frac{1}{4}$ cup ($\frac{1}{2}$ stick) unsalted butter
$\frac{3}{4}$ cup plus 2 tablespoons firmly packed light brown sugar
1 teaspoon finely grated orange rind
1 egg
$\frac{1}{4}$ cup buttermilk
2 tablespoons wheat germ
$1\frac{1}{4}$ cups sifted all-purpose flour
$\frac{1}{2}$ teaspoon baking soda
  Pinch ground cinnamon
  Pinch salt
$\frac{3}{4}$ teaspoon vanilla

Cream the butter with the brown sugar and orange rind until light; beat in the egg, then stir in the buttermilk and wheat germ. Combine the flour, soda, cinnamon and salt and mix into the dough; finally, stir in the vanilla. Drop the cookies from a $\frac{1}{2}$ teaspoon measure onto baking sheets lightly sprayed with non-stick vegetable cooking spray, spacing them $1\frac{1}{2}$″ apart. Bake in a hot oven (400°F.) for 10 minutes, then lift at once to wire racks to cool. 29 calories per cookie.

CHOCOLATE HAZELNUT MERINGUES
Makes 4½ Dozen

Spicy and crisp and just 17 calories apiece. Delicious with fresh peaches, plums, berries or melon.

NOTE: Do not attempt to make these cookies in humid or rainy weather because they will absorb atmospheric moisture and become gummy.

    5 large egg whites
    1 cup sifted confectioners' (10X) sugar
    ¼ teaspoon ground cinnamon
    1 square (1 ounce) semisweet chocolate, very finely
       grated

NOTE: The chocolate will grate much more easily if it is ice-cold.
    ¼ cup finely ground toasted blanched hazelnuts or
       almonds
    ½ teaspoon vanilla

Beat egg whites until frothy; add 2 tablespoons of the 10X sugar and beat until silvery. Now continue adding the sugar gradually, beating all the while, until mixture is very stiff. Beat in the cinnamon, then gently but thoroughly fold in the chocolate, hazelnuts and vanilla.

Drop the meringues from rounded teaspoonfuls onto baking sheets that have been lined with aluminum foil (the shiny side of the foil should be down). Bake in a very slow oven (250°F.) for about 3 hours—just until the meringues feel firm to the touch and are a nice golden tan. Remove from the oven, cool briefly, then transfer the meringues to wire racks to cool.

NOTE: If you twist the meringues gently; they will pop right off the foil. Store in an airtight cannister. 17 calories per meringue.

PRALINE PUFFS
Makes 3½ Dozen

Perfect puffs for praline lovers. It is imperative that you choose a dry, sunny day on which to make these melt-in-your-mouth cookies. In rainy or muggy weather, they will hydrolize (absorb atmospheric moisture) and become unpleasantly gummy.

    4 large egg whites
    ⅛ teaspoon salt
    ¼ cup unsifted confectioners' (10X) sugar
    8 tablespoons light brown sugar
    1½ teaspoons vanilla
    1 teaspoon lemon juice
    ½ teaspoon maple flavoring

Beat the egg whites with the salt until frothy; add half of the 10X sugar and beat until silvery; add the remaining 10X sugar and beat just until the eggs begin to stiffen. Now add the brown sugar, a tablespoon at a time, beating all the while. Drizzle the vanilla, lemon juice and maple flavoring over the beaten whites and continue beating until very stiff and dry.

NOTE: The whites should be so stiff that if you slash a knife through them, it will leave a crisp, clean cut.

Quickly line 3 baking sheets with aluminum foil, placing the dull side up. Drop the meringue mixture by well-mounded teaspoonfuls onto the baking sheets, placing the cookies about 1½" apart. Bake in a very slow oven (250°F.) for 1 hour, turn the oven off and leave the cookies in the oven until it is cold. To remove the cookies from the foil, twist lightly; store in an airtight cannister. 13 calories per cookie.

SPICY APPLE-WALNUT BARS
Makes 16

For the fruit and nut lover. Use a light touch in mixing these bar cookies, otherwise they may toughen.

- 1 large egg
- $\frac{1}{2}$ cup firmly packed light brown sugar
- 1 large tart green apple, peeled, cored and chopped (you should have $\frac{3}{4}$ to 1 cup chopped apple)
- $\frac{3}{4}$ cup unsifted self-rising cake flour
- $\frac{1}{4}$ teaspoon ground cinnamon
- $\frac{1}{4}$ teaspoon ground nutmeg
- $\frac{1}{8}$ teaspoon ground ginger
- $\frac{1}{2}$ teaspoon vanilla
- $\frac{1}{3}$ cup walnuts, chopped fine

Beat the egg and sugar hard until creamy; stir in the apple. Combine the flour with the cinnamon, nutmeg and ginger and stir into the apple mixture along with the vanilla and walnuts.

Spoon into an 8″ x 8″ x 2″ baking pan that has been liberally sprayed with nonstick vegetable cooking spray and smooth the top with a rubber spatula. Bake in a moderate oven (350°F.) for 20 to 25 minutes or until springy to the touch and the mixture begins to pull from the sides of the pan.

Remove from the oven and cool upright in the pan on a wire rack for 30 minutes. Cut into 16 squares of equal size and serve. 68 calories per bar.

FUDGY BROWNIES
Makes 16

Dense, dark and delicious. Best of all, these contain just 97 calories apiece. If this doesn't seem low calorie to you, consider for a moment the chocoholic's favorite, which averages better than 350 *per* brownie. How, then, were the calories shaved so drastically here? I substituted cocoa for chocolate, also heavy cream for butter (it contains 50 percent fewer calories), then made it do double duty, serving as both shortening and liquid.

5 tablespoons cocoa powder (not a mix)
5 tablespoons sugar
8 packets (1 gram each) aspartame sweetener
2 tablespoons cornstarch
$\frac{2}{3}$ cup unsifted self-rising cake flour
1 large egg, lightly beaten
$\frac{3}{4}$ cup heavy cream
$\frac{1}{4}$ cup evaporated milk
$1\frac{1}{2}$ teaspoons vanilla

In a medium-size mixing bowl, combine the cocoa, sugar, sweetener, cornstarch and flour, pressing out all lumps; make a well in the center of the dry ingredients and set aside for the moment. Combine the egg, heavy cream, evaporated milk and vanilla in a small bowl, whisking until smooth; dump into the well in the dry ingredients, then mix briskly and lightly to form a thin batter. Do not overbeat at this point or you will toughen the brownies (no matter if there are a few lumps in the batter; they will disappear during baking).

Pour into an 8″ x 8″ x 2″ baking pan that has been sprayed with nonstick vegetable cooking spray and bake in a moderate oven (350°F.) for 20 to 25 minutes—just until the brownies feel soft-firm and begin to pull from the sides of the pan. Cool upright in the pan on a wire rack to room temperature, then cut into 16 squares of equal size. 97 calories per brownie.

TART ORANGE FILLING
Makes about 1⅔ Cups

Spoon this sunny filling over slices of sponge or angel food cake or use to fill Chocolate-Orange-Pecan Torte (see p. 144). This filling is also very good stirred into fruit compotes or mixed with sliced peaches or strawberries. In other words, it's handy to have on hand. Stored tightly covered in the refrigerator, it keeps well for about a week.

    1½ cups freshly squeezed orange juice
    1 teaspoon finely grated orange rind
    2 teaspoons plain gelatin
    2 large egg yolks, lightly beaten
    1 tablespoon unsalted butter
    4 packets (1 gram each) aspartame sweetener

Place the orange juice and rind in a small heavy enameled or stainless steel saucepan; sprinkle the gelatin evenly over the surface, set over moderate heat and stir 3 to 4 minutes until the gelatin is completely dissolved. Whisk a little of the hot mixture into the egg yolks, stir back into the pan and heat and stir 1 to 2 minutes. Remove from the heat and stir in the butter; cool to room temperature, then mix in the sweetener. Pour into a small bowl, cover tight and store in the refrigerator. 429 calories total or 16 calories per tablespoon.

CRÈME PATISSIÈRE (CLASSIC PASTRY CREAM)
Makes 2 Cups

Use this pastry cream (or any of its variations below) for filling cream puffs and éclairs; you'll find low-calorie versions of both (see pp. 48 and 49).

> 1 cup milk
> 1 cup skim milk
> 3 tablespoons cornstarch
> 3 large egg yolks, lightly beaten
> 10 packets (1 gram each) aspartame sweetener
> 2 teaspoons vanilla

In a large shaker jar with a tight-fitting lid, combine the milk, skim milk and cornstarch by shaking vigorously (or you can buzz these three ingredients up in a food processor fitted with the metal chopping blade). Dump into a small heavy saucepan, set over moderate heat and whisk vigorously 3 to 4 minutes, just until the mixture bubbles up and thickens (it will be quite stiff); whisk a little of the hot mixture into the egg yolks, stir back into pan and whisk for 1 minute. Remove from the heat, set the pan in an ice bath and whisk frequently until the pastry cream cools to room temperature. Blend in the sweetener and vanilla, then transfer to a small bowl, cover and chill about 1 hour before using. 17 calories per tablespoon.

Variations:

Crème Patissière au Chocolat (Chocolate Pastry Cream): In a large shaker jar with a tight-fitting lid, combine the milk, skim milk and cornstarch (above) with 3 tablespoons cocoa powder (not a mix) by shaking vigorously. Proceed as recipe directs. 20 calories per tablespoon.

Crème Patissière au Citron (Lemon Pastry Cream): Prepare as directed above but omit the vanilla; flavor instead with 2 teaspoons lemon juice and the finely grated rind of 1 lemon; increase the amount of aspartame sweetener to 12 packets (1 gram each). 17 calories per tablespoon.

Crème Patissière à l'Orange (Orange Pastry Cream): **Prepare the pastry cream as directed above, but omit the vanilla; flavor instead with 2 teaspoons of orange juice and 1 teaspoon finely grated orange rind. 17 calories per tablespoon.**

NOTE: If you prefer, flavor with 1 tablespoon Grand Marnier and 1 teaspoon finely grated orange rind; 19 calories per tablespoon.

6
DESSERT SAUCES AND TOPPINGS

CRÈME ANGLAISE
Makes about 2½ Cups

This silky custard sauce is delicious over fresh berries, sliced oranges or peaches or Burgundy-Poached Pears (see p. 111). It is also superb ladled over sponge or angel cake.

1 cup evaporated skim milk
1 cup milk
¼ cup half-and-half cream
2 tablespoons cornstarch
2 large egg yolks, lightly beaten
6 packets (1 gram each) aspartame sweetener
1½ teaspoons vanilla

Place the evaporated skim milk and milk in a small heavy saucepan; blend the half-and-half with the cornstarch to make a smooth paste and mix into pan. Set over moderate heat and cook and stir 2 to 3 minutes, just until mixture thickens. Whisk a little of the hot sauce into the yolks, stir back into pan and cook and stir about 1 minute longer. Remove from the heat and cool almost to room temperature, whisking often to prevent a skin from forming on the surface of the sauce. Mix in the sweetener and vanilla, pour into a bowl, cover and refrigerate until ready to serve. 16 calories per tablespoon.

ORANGE ZABAGLIONE SAUCE
Makes 1½ Cups

This billowing sauce isn't difficult to make and it adds considerable drama (but few calories) to fresh sliced peaches, oranges, apricots or strawberries. Try it, too, spooned over ripe whole red raspberries or blueberries, over slices of sponge cake or wedges of Angel Ring à la Algarve (see p. 197).

> 4 large egg yolks
> ½ cup unsifted confectioners' (10X) sugar
> ½ cup freshly squeezed orange juice
> 1 teaspoon Grand Marnier
> ½ teaspoon finely grated orange rind

In a double boiler top, beat the egg yolks until foamy. Add the 10X sugar gradually, beating hard all the while; now drizzle in the orange juice, beating hard; finally beat in the Grand Marnier and orange rind.

Set over just-simmering water and continue beating hard for 6 to 8 minutes until the zabaglione thickens, billows and more than triples in volume.

NOTE: Do not let the water in the bottom part of the double boiler boil at any time or the mixture may curdle.

As soon as the zabaglione is about the consistency of softly whipped cream and no longer tastes of raw egg, remove from the heat. Serve warm, or cool to room temperature, whisk hard and serve. 21 calories per tablespoon.

FRESH ORANGE SAUCE
Makes 2¼ Cups

Very good over orange or lemon sherbet, sponge or angel cake.
I also very much like this sauce ladled over sliced navel oranges.

2 cups freshly squeezed orange juice
3 tablespoons cornstarch
¼ cup lemon juice
  Rind of 1 orange, cut into fine julienne (use the zest
    or orange part only)
1 teaspoon unsalted butter
1 tablespoon Grand Marnier
6 packets (1 gram each) aspartame sweetener

Combine the orange juice and cornstarch in a small, heavy
saucepan (not aluminum, which may give the filling a metallic
taste), stirring until the cornstarch is completely dissolved in the
orange juice. Set over moderately low heat and whisk constantly
3 to 4 minutes until the mixture bubbles up and clears. Off the
heat, stir in the lemon juice, orange rind and butter. Cool to
room temperature, whisking now and then to prevent a skin
from forming on the surface of the sauce; mix in the Grand
Marnier and sweetener. 11 calories per tablespoon.

NIPPY LEMON SAUCE
Makes 2 Cups

I like this sauce best over fresh sliced oranges or peaches, but it is very good, too, over slices of a sponge or angel cake.

1½ cups water
 2 tablespoons plus 2 teaspoons cornstarch
   Juice of 2 large lemons
   Rind of 1 large lemon, grated fine
 1 tablespoon unsalted butter
16 packets (1 gram each) aspartame sweetener

In a small heavy saucepan (not aluminum, which may make the sauce taste metallic), combine the water and cornstarch until completely uniform; set over moderately low heat and whisk constantly 3 to 4 minutes—just until the mixture bubbles up, thickens and clears. Remove from the heat at once, mix in the lemon juice, rind and butter. Cool to room temperature, whisking occasionally lest a skin form on the surface of the sauce; mix in the sweetener, then serve. 8 calories per tablespoon.

ALBUFEIRA APRICOT SAUCE
Makes 1½ Cups

In Portugal's Algarve Province, where I first tasted this light and lemony sauce some years ago, fresh apricots were used because they grow abundantly in this sunwashed land. I have taken the liberty of substituting canned apricots but, take note, they are *unsweetened,* water-packed apricots.

1 can (1 pound) unsweetened, water-pack apricot halves
   (do not drain)
3 tablespoons water
½ cinnamon stick
2 strips (each about 2″ x ½″) lemon rind (yellow part
   only)
1 teaspoon unsalted butter
6 packets (1 gram each) aspartame sweetener (about)

Puree the apricots with their juice by buzzing in a food processor fitted with the metal chopping blade or in an electric blender at high speed or by forcing through a food mill. Dump into a small heavy saucepan (not aluminum), add the water, cinnamon stick and lemon rind and simmer uncovered over moderately low heat 35 to 40 minutes until reduced by about one-fourth; stir occasionally to prevent sticking or scorching. Off heat, stir in the butter. Cool to room temperature, remove the cinnamon stick and lemon rind, then blend in the sweetener. Serve over Angel Ring à la Algarve (see p. 197), over sliced fresh peaches, apricots or oranges or ladle over sponge or angel food cake. 10 calories per tablespoon.

PEACH GRAND MARNIER SAUCE
Makes 2 Cups

Spoon over fresh sliced peaches or oranges, over angel or sponge cake. Or try ladling this sauce over Angel Ring à la Algarve (see p. 197). Ambrosia!

> 2 packages (10 ounces each) quick-thaw frozen sliced peaches
> 1 tablespoon lemon juice
> 1 teaspoon unsalted butter
> 1 tablespoon Grand Marnier

Partially thaw the peaches, then puree by buzzing in a food processor fitted with the metal chopping blade or in an electric blender cup—three to four 30-second churnings should be sufficient.

NOTE: If you have neither blender nor food processor, you will have to thaw the peaches completely, then puree by forcing through a food mill. Pour into a small heavy saucepan (preferably stainless steel, flameproof glass or enameled cast iron so that the sauce doesn't take on a metallic taste), set over very low heat and reduce by simmering uncovered for 30 minutes. Stir now and then to prevent the mixture from scorching. Remove from the heat, add the butter, cool 10 minutes, then stir in the Grand Marnier. Pour into a 1-pint preserving jar, cover and store in the refrigerator. 19 calories per tablespoon.

NUTMEG SAUCE
Makes 1 Cup

Not the usual dessert sauce but an unusually good one. Spoon over fresh sliced peaches, baked apples or sponge cake.

NOTE: You must use freshly grated nutmeg for this recipe; the commercially ground will make the sauce taste bitter.

> 1 tablespoon cornstarch
> ½ teaspoon *freshly grated* nutmeg
> Juice of ½ lemon
> 1 cup water
> 1 tablespoon unsalted butter
> 6 to 8 packets (1 gram each) aspartame sweetener (or to taste)

In a 1-pint jar with a screw top, place the cornstarch, nutmeg, lemon juice and water. Shake hard until absolutely smooth. Pour into a small heavy saucepan, set over moderate heat and stir 3 to 4 minutes, just until the mixture bubbles up once, thickens and clears. Off the heat, stir in the butter. Cool to lukewarm, then mix in enough sweetener to taste. Serve warm. 7 calories per tablespoon.

EASY MELBA SAUCE
Makes 2½ Cups

I can't think of a more dazzling or delicious way to dress up fresh sliced peaches, apricots or oranges. This sauce is equally good ladled over fruit ice or sherbet, even sponge or angel food cake.

> 1 package (10 ounces) quick-thaw frozen raspberries
> 1 package (10 ounces) quick-thaw frozen strawberries
> 1 tablespoon Cointreau

Partially thaw both packages of berries (about 20 minutes at room temperature should be sufficient). Dump the berries and all of their juices into a food processor fitted with the metal chopping blade or into an electric blender and buzz until uniformly pureed. Add the Cointreau and buzz for another minute or so.

NOTE: If you have neither processor nor blender, force the berries through a food mill, then mix in the Cointreau.

Press the puree through a fine sieve to extract the berry seeds, then pour into a glass jar and store in the refrigerator.

NOTE: Use within 2 to 3 days. 15 calories per tablespoon.

QUICK CARDINAL SAUCE
Makes 2½ Cups

Simply splendid over sliced fresh apricots, oranges, peaches, any fruit sherbet or mousse.

- 1 package (10 ounces) quick-thaw frozen raspberries
- 1 tablespoon Kirsch
- 1 pint ripe strawberries, washed, hulled and sliced thin
- 5 packets (1 gram each) aspartame sweetener

Partially thaw the raspberries, then puree by buzzing in an electric blender at high speed or in a food processor equipped with the metal chopping blade; press through a fine sieve to remove seeds, then mix with the Kirsch and set aside.

Place the strawberries in a medium-size mixing bowl, sprinkle the sweetener evenly over all, toss well and let stand at room temperature 10 minutes. Stir in the reserved pureed raspberries, then chill about 1 hour before serving. 12 calories per tablespoon.

BUTTERSCOTCH SAUCE
Makes 2 Cups

This sauce and the one that follows are delicious served warm over ice milk, angel food or sponge cake. They're also superb ladled over Angel Ring à la Algarve (see p. 197).

> $\frac{1}{4}$ cup firmly packed light brown sugar
> $\frac{1}{4}$ cup firmly packed dark brown sugar
> 2 tablespoons cornstarch
> 1$\frac{1}{2}$ cups water
> $\frac{1}{2}$ cup evaporated milk
> 2 teaspoons butter
> 1$\frac{1}{2}$ teaspoons vanilla
> 4 to 6 teaspoons cider vinegar (enough to add a touch of tartness)

In a small heavy saucepan, combine the light and dark brown sugars and cornstarch, pressing out all lumps. Mix in the water and evaporated milk.

NOTE: If the brown sugars are very lumpy, buzz them with the cornstarch, water and evaporated milk in an electric blender at high speed or in a food processor fitted with the metal chopping blade; pour mixture into saucepan. Set over moderate heat and stir 3 to 4 minutes, just until mixture bubbles up once and thickens. Remove from the heat, stir in the butter, vanilla and just enough cider vinegar to temper the sweetness of the sauce. Serve warm or at room temperature. 22 calories per tablespoon.

CREAMY CARAMEL SAUCE
Makes 2 Cups

Another delicious sauce over cake or ice cream.

$\frac{1}{4}$ cup firmly packed dark brown sugar
2 tablespoons cornstarch
2 cups evaporated skim milk
1 teaspoon unsalted butter
1$\frac{1}{2}$ teaspoons vanilla
2 teaspoons lemon juice

Combine the sugar and cornstarch in a small heavy saucepan, pressing out all lumps. Mix in the evaporated skim milk, set over moderate heat and stir 3 to 4 minutes, just until the mixture bubbles up and thickens. Remove from the heat and stir in the butter, vanilla and lemon juice. Serve warm or at room temperature. 22 calories per tablespoon.

BITTERSWEET CHOCOLATE SAUCE
Makes 2 Cups

With regular chocolate sauce averaging 85 calories per table-spoon and hot fudge sauce 100, this one's a true caloric bargain and the one that follows is a miracle.

    3 tablespoons sugar
    4 tablespoons cocoa powder (not a mix)
    4 tablespoons all-purpose flour
    1 cup evaporated milk
    1 cup skim milk
    1½ teaspoons vanilla
    1 teaspoon unsalted butter

In a small heavy saucepan, combine the sugar, cocoa and flour, pressing out all lumps. Mix in the evaporated milk and skim milk, set over moderate heat and whisk and cook 3 to 4 minutes until sauce thickens. Remove from the heat and stir in vanilla and butter. Serve hot over cake or ice cream or cool to room temperature before serving.

NOTE: To prevent a skin from forming on the surface of the sauce as it cools, whisk from time to time. Store the sauce in the refrigerator in a tightly covered bowl or jar and stir well before using. 26 calories per tablespoon.

HOT FUDGE SAUCE
Makes 1½ Cups

How can anything so rich, dark and thick be so low in calories? I have added no sugar at all, substituted cocoa for chocolate, then brought the calorie count down still further by using evaporated skim milk and lowfat buttermilk, both of which are marvelously creamy.

3 tablespoons cocoa powder (not a mix)
4 teaspoons cornstarch
¾ cup lowfat buttermilk
¾ cup evaporated skim milk
6 packets (1 gram each) aspartame sweetener
1 teaspoon vanilla

In a small heavy saucepan, combine the cocoa and cornstarch, pressing out all lumps; whisk in the buttermilk, then the evaporated skim milk. When completely uniform, set over moderately low heat and whisk 3 to 4 minutes until mixture bubbles up and thickens. Remove from the heat, cool 3 to 4 minutes, whisk in the sweetener and vanilla and serve over French Chocolate Ice Cream, Angel Food Cake or Celestial Marble Cake (see pp. 93, 133 and 135). 12 calories per tablespoon.

LOW-CALORIE WHIPPED "CREAM"
Makes 2 Cups

I cannot in all honesty pretend that this is as good as the real thing, but when you consider that it contains only one-tenth of the calories of genuine whipped cream, I think you will find it a very good substitute.

NOTE: This whipped "cream" will deflate soon after it's whipped, so do not prepare it ahead of time.

$\frac{1}{3}$ cup ice water
$\frac{1}{3}$ cup nonfat dry milk powder
2 packets (1 gram each) aspartame sweetener
4 teaspoons lemon juice
$\frac{1}{2}$ teaspoon vanilla

Place the water in a small bowl and sprinkle in the milk powder and sweetener. With an electric beater set at high speed, whip until frothy. Add a teaspoon of the lemon juice and continue beating at high speed until the cream begins to thicken; add another teaspoon of lemon juice and beat hard to soft peaks; add the final 2 teaspoons of lemon juice and beat to stiff peaks.

NOTE: You will find that this mixture whips up much more slowly than heavy cream, so do not become discouraged. Beat in the vanilla, then serve in place of whipped cream. 3 calories per tablespoon.

Variation:

Crème Chantilly: Prepare as directed but omit the vanilla. When the milk has been whipped to stiff peaks, fold in 1 tablespoon brandy or Armagnac. 5 calories per tablespoon.

MOCK DEVONSHIRE CREAM
Makes 5 Cups

Superb spooned over any fresh berries, also over fresh sliced peaches, plums, nectarines or figs.

    1 pint half-and-half cream
    1½ teaspoons plain gelatin
    1 cup evaporated skim milk
    8 packets (1 gram each) aspartame sweetener
    1½ cups plain yogurt
    1 teaspoon vanilla

Pour the half-and-half into a medium-size heavy saucepan, sprinkle the gelatin evenly over the surface and let stand several minutes. Set over moderate heat and stir 3 to 4 minutes until gelatin dissolves completely. Remove from the heat, stir in the evaporated skim milk and cool to room temperature. Mix in the sweetener, then the yogurt and vanilla. Cover and chill several hours until as thick as clotted cream.

NOTE: Stored tightly covered in the refrigerator, the Mock Devonshire Cream will keep well for 4 to 5 days. 14 calories per tablespoon (as compared with 53 for heavy cream and 28 for sour cream).

NATURAL FRUIT GLAZE
Makes ½ Cup

Nothing more than a two-to-one mixture of unsweetened apple juice and cranberry juice cocktail boiled down to the consistency of syrup, this glaze adds a rosy blush to open-face fruit tarts and baked apples. Use it, too, to sweeten fruit compotes, fresh berries, sliced fresh peaches and apricots.

    1 cup unsweetened apple juice
    ½ cup cranberry juice cocktail

Place both ingredients in a small heavy saucepan (not aluminum, which might give the glaze a metallic taste) and bring to a simmer over moderate heat. Adjust the heat so that the mixture bubbles *very* lazily, then cook, uncovered, about 1 hour until reduced to ½ cup. Stir from time to time and watch the "pot" carefully lest the mixture scorch. 189 calories total; 24 calories per tablespoon.

PINEAPPLE-GINGER CHEESECAKE TOPPING

Makes about 1 Cup

Use as a topping for Light and Lovely Lemon Cheesecake (see p. 40).

1 can (8 ounces) crushed pineapple packed in
    unsweetened pineapple juice
3 tablespoons sugar
1 tablespoon cornstarch
    Pinch ground ginger

Combine all ingredients in a small saucepan, bring to a boil over moderate heat, stirring all the while. Boil 1 minute until mixture thickens and clears, then remove from the heat and cool to room temperature. Spread on top of chilled cheesecake. Added calories to each of 12 servings of cheesecake: 22.

CHERRY CHEESECAKE TOPPING
Makes about 1½ Cups

Use as a topping for Light and Lovely Lemon Cheesecake or Mocha Cheesecake (see pp. 40 and 42).

> 1 can (16 ounces) water-pack pitted sour red cherries, drained
> 2 tablespoons sugar
> 4½ teaspoons cornstarch
> ½ cup cranberry juice cocktail
> ½ teaspoon almond extract
> ¼ teaspoon vanilla
> 2 to 3 drops red food coloring (optional)
> 1 drop yellow food coloring (optional)

Dump the cherries into a heatproof bowl and set aside. Combine the sugar and cornstarch in a small heavy saucepan, blend in the cranberry juice, bring to a boil over moderate heat, stirring all the while, then let mixture boil 1 minute until thickened and clear. Pour over the cherries, add almond extract, vanilla and, if you like, just enough red and yellow food coloring to give the cherries a nice red hue. Cool to room temperature, then spread on top of chilled cheesecake. Added calories to each of 12 servings of cheesecake: 34.

CRAN-APPLE CHEESECAKE TOPPING
Makes about 1½ Cups

Spread over Light and Lovely Lemon Cheesecake (see p. 40). Or use as a topper for any favorite cheesecake.

⅓ cup sugar
¼ cup plus 1 teaspoon water
1 cup fresh cranberries, washed and stemmed
½ cup chopped, peeled tart apple
2 teaspoons cornstarch
1 teaspoon lemon juice

In a small saucepan set over moderate heat, bring the sugar and ¼ cup of the water to a boil; as soon as the sugar is dissolved, add the cranberries and apple and cook uncovered, stirring now and then, 5 minutes. Meanwhile, blend the cornstarch, lemon juice and remaining 1 teaspoon water. Stir into the cranberry mixture, bubble for 1 minute until thickened and clear. Remove from the heat and cool to room temperature. Spread on top of chilled cheesecake. Added calories to each of 12 servings of cheesecake: 29.

7
SHOWSTOPPERS (LAVISH PARTY DESSERTS)

DACQUOISE (LAYERED MERINGUE TORTE WITH MOCHA-HAZELNUT FILLING)

Serves 12

Guaranteed to dazzle dinner guests, this lavish dessert contains only 141 calories per serving (compare *that* to the 530 calories of an all-stops-out dacquoise). The difference? A true dacquoise is a triple-decker sandwich of hazelnut-studded meringues and butter-cream filling. I think this low-calorie version is every bit as good, and like a true dacquoise, it can be made several days ahead of time and stored in the freezer. Let the dacquoise stand at room temperature about 15 minutes before cutting and serving.

1 recipe Meringue Layers (see p. 54)

Filling:

> 2 tablespoons Dutch-process cocoa powder (not a mix)
> 2 tablespoons sugar
> 2 teaspoons gelatin
> 2 cups evaporated skim milk
> 2 egg yolks, lightly beaten
> 1 teaspoon freeze-dried coffee crystals
> 1½ teaspoons vanilla
> 1 package (3 ounces) cream cheese, cut into small bits and brought to room temperature
> 6 packets (1 gram each) aspartame sweetener
> ½ teaspoon hazelnut oil

Prepare the meringue layers as directed and keep in the turned-off oven until you are ready to assemble the dacquoise.

For the Filling: In a small heavy saucepan, combine the cocoa, sugar and gelatin, pressing out any lumps. Pour in the milk, set over moderate heat and stir 3 to 4 minutes until the gelatin dissolves completely. Whisk a little of the hot mixture into the yolks, stir back into the pan, then cook and stir over low heat 1 to 2 minutes until slightly thickened (do not allow to boil or mixture may curdle). Off heat, stir in the coffee, vanilla and cream cheese. Whisk until the cream cheese melts and the mixture is as satiny as chocolate pudding. Mix in the sweetener.

Pour into a metal bowl and quick-chill in the freezer until thick and syrupy. Beat hard in an electric mixer at high speed until creamy smooth. Quick-chill again until about the consistency of chocolate pudding; whisk in the hazelnut oil, then return briefly to the freezer until of a good spreading consistency.

To Assemble the Dacquoise: Place one of the smooth-surfaced meringues on a large round cake plate; spread with half of the filling and top with the second smooth-surfaced meringue, pressing it ever so lightly into the filling. If the filling seems to be softening too much to spread, set both it and the partially assembled dacquoise in the freezer until the filling firms up again. Spread the remaining filling on the dacquoise, then top with the third meringue, arranging the roughened-surface up so that the relief shows. Press the top meringue lightly into the filling. Return the dacquoise to the freezer and freeze until firm. Now wrap snugly—plate and all—in several thicknesses of plastic food wrap (to seal out all freezer odors). Store in the freezer until shortly before you're ready to serve.

NOTE: The dacquoise will keep well in the freezer for a week to ten days.

To Serve the Dacquoise: Remove the dacquoise from the freezer and unwrap. Let stand on the counter about 15 minutes—just until the filling softens enough to slice through it easily. Using a very sharp serrated knife dipped in hot water, cut the dacquoise into 12 pieces of equal size.

NOTE: You'll have to dip the knife into hot water before each cut so keep a saucepan of it handy. 141 calories per serving.

VACHERIN AUX FRAMBOISES (RASPBERRY MERINGUE TORTE)

Serves 12

I first tasted this spectacular dessert at a little inn high above the French Riviera, never dreaming that it was low in calories. Truth to tell, that dessert wasn't nearly as low in calories as this equally tempting version of it, which contains just 110 calories per opulent portion.

NOTE: This dessert, like any other based on meringue, should be made on a perfectly dry day.

1 recipe Meringue Layers (see p. 54)

Raspberry Filling:

- 2 packages (10 ounces each) quick-thaw frozen raspberries
- ⅔ cup water
- 1 envelope plain gelatin
- 1 tablespoon lemon juice
- 2 packets (1 gram each) aspartame sweetener
- 1 tablespoon framboise (raspberry *eau de vie*)

Prepare the meringue layers as directed and keep in the turned-off oven until you are ready to assemble the vacherin.

For the Filling: Partially thaw the raspberries, puree by buzzing in an electric blender at high speed or in a food processor fitted with the metal chopping blade or by forcing through a food mill. Sieve the puree to remove seeds; pour into a small mixing bowl and set aside.

Place the water in a very small heavy saucepan, sprinkle the gelatin over the surface and let stand a minute or two; set over moderately low heat and stir 2 to 3 minutes, just until the gelatin is completely dissolved. Stir the gelatin into the puree along with all remaining filling ingredients. Freeze until mushy firm, beat at high mixer speed (or whir in a food processor fitted with the metal chopping blade) until fluffy light.

To Assemble the Vacherin: Place one of the smooth-surfaced meringues on a large round cake plate; spread with half of the filling and top with the second smooth-surfaced meringue, pressing it ever so lightly into the filling. If the filling seems to be softening too much to spread, set both it and the partially assembled vacherin in the freezer until the filling firms up again. Spread the remaining filling on the second meringue layer, then top with the third meringue layer, arranging it roughened-surface up so that the relief shows. Press the top meringue lightly into the filling. Return the vacherin to the freezer and freeze until firm. Now wrap snugly—plate and all—in several thicknesses of plastic food wrap (to seal out freezer odors). Store in the freezer until shortly before you're ready to serve.

NOTE: The vacherin will keep well in the freezer for about a month.

To Serve the Vacherin: Remove the vacherin from the freezer and unwrap. Let stand on the counter 15 to 20 minutes—just until the raspberry filling softens sufficiently to be sliced easily. Using a sharp serrated knife dipped in hot water, cut the vacherin into 12 wedges of equal size.

NOTE: You'll have to dip the knife into hot water before each cut so keep a saucepan of it at hand. 110 calories per serving.

PAVLOVA
Serves 6

This theatrical red, white and green dessert was dreamed up by an enterprising Australian chef in honor of the famous Russian prima ballerina.

NOTE: If the meringue is to be properly shattery-crisp, you must make it on a dry sunny day.

Meringue:

4 large egg whites, at room temperature
Pinch salt
Pinch cream of tartar
$\frac{1}{4}$ cup unsifted confectioners' (10X) sugar
$\frac{1}{3}$ cup superfine sugar
$\frac{1}{4}$ teaspoon vanilla

Custard Cream:

1 cup milk
1 cup skim milk
1 vanilla bean, sliced lengthwise
3 tablespoons cornstarch
2 large egg yolks, lightly beaten
6 packets (1 gram each) aspartame sweetener
$\frac{1}{2}$ teaspoon vanilla

Fruit Topping:

1 cup ripe strawberries, washed, hulled, sliced and patted very dry on paper toweling
2 medium-size kiwi fruits, peeled and sliced very thin crosswise

Glaze:

1 cup cran-apple juice, boiled hard until reduced to $\frac{1}{3}$ cup

For the Meringue: Line a baking sheet with aluminum foil, placing the dull-side up, then trace an 8″ circle in the center of the foil (use an 8″ layer-cake pan as a pattern). Whip the egg whites with the salt and cream of tartar until frothy; continue beating the whites, adding first the 10X sugar, then the superfine, 1 tablespoon at a time, until all sugar has been incorporated and the whites are very stiff and dry. If you slash a knife through the meringue, the cut-edge should hold crisp and firm. Beat in the vanilla, then spoon the meringue into a large pastry bag fitted with a large plain tip. Pipe the meringue onto the traced circle on the cookie sheet in a spiral or coil pattern, then pipe a 1″ rim around the edge of the meringue circle.

Bake the meringue in a very slow oven (250°F.) for 1 hour, then turn the oven off and let the meringue dry out in the oven for a few hours or overnight.

For the Custard Cream: Pour all of the milk and all but 3 tablespoons of the skim milk into a high-sided, heavy saucepan, drop in the vanilla bean and bring the milk just to the scalding point. Turn the heat off and allow the bean to steep in the milk 1 hour. Scrape the inside of the bean (tiny black seeds) into the milk and discard the pod. Mix the cornstarch with the 3 tablespoons of skim milk you've set aside, blend into the saucepan, set over moderate heat and cook, whisking constantly, just until the mixture bubbles up and thickens. Whisk a little of the hot mixture into the yolks, stir back into pan and whisk and stir 1 minute (do not allow to boil or the custard may curdle). Remove from the heat, transfer to a heatproof bowl and cool to room temperature, whisking often to prevent a skin from forming on the surface of the custard; blend in the sweetener and vanilla.

To Assemble the Pavlova: Spoon the custard into the meringue shell, arrange the sliced strawberries and kiwis on top in a pretty pattern (concentric circles, for example, or pie-shaped wedges). Using a pastry brush, paint the fruit carefully with the hot glaze—if the glaze is too sticky to spread easily, thin with a little hot water.

Cut into 6 wedges and serve immediately.

NOTE: The last-minute assembly goes very fast if you have everything ready, so the guests won't have to wait for their Pavlova. 195 calories per serving.

STRAWBERRY CHIFFON CHARLOTTE

Serves 8

A scrumptious strawberry dessert. You can, if you like, substitute other fresh pureed fruit for the strawberries as the variations below so deliciously prove.

1 recipe Ladyfingers (see p. 151)

Strawberry Chiffon Filling:

$1\frac{1}{2}$ cups pureed dead-ripe strawberries (for this amount you'll need 1 pint strawberries)
1 envelope plus 2 teaspoons plain gelatin
4 tablespoons sugar
2 tablespoons orange juice
2 large egg whites
$\frac{1}{4}$ teaspoon cream of tartar
$\frac{1}{2}$ cup ice-cold evaporated skim milk

Optional Garnishes:

10 to 12 perfect ripe strawberries
3 to 4 sprigs of mint, rose geranium or lemon verbena
1 tablespoon confectioners' (10X) sugar

Prepare ladyfingers as directed. Spray the bottom and sides of an 8″ springform pan with nonstick vegetable cooking spray, then stand ladyfingers on end and just touching one another around the sides of the pan. Cover the bottom of the pan with the remaining ladyfingers, cutting them as needed to fit and fill in the spaces.

NOTE: It doesn't matter if your design is less than perfect or if ladyfingers completely cover the bottom of the pan; the charlotte will not be inverted. Set the pan aside while you prepare the filling.

For the Strawberry Chiffon Filling: In a small heavy saucepan combine the strawberry puree, the 1 envelope gelatin and 2 tablespoons of the sugar. Set over moderate heat and stir until gelatin and sugar both dissolve—3 to 4 minutes. Cool mixture, then quick-chill until syrupy by setting in the freezer. In a tiny saucepan or butter warmer (*not* unlined copper), combine the orange juice and remaining 2 teaspoons of gelatin. Stir over moderate heat 1 to 2 minutes until gelatin dissolves; cool. Beat the egg whites with the cream of tartar to soft peaks; beat in the remaining sugar, 1 tablespoon at a time, then continue beating until the meringue forms stiff peaks.

Now whip the evaporated skim milk at high mixer speed until it begins to thicken. Add the orange-juice mixture and continue beating until fluffy and stiff.

Beat the chilled strawberry mixture until frothy, then gently but thoroughly fold in the meringue; dump this mixture on top of the whipped evaporated milk and fold in lightly until no streaks of pink or white remain. Pour the strawberry chiffon into the ladyfinger-lined pan, cover loosely and refrigerate for at least 3 hours.

To serve, carefully loosen and remove the springform-pan sides and set the charlotte, still on the pan bottom, on a decorative dessert plate. Garnish, if you like, with clusters of perfect strawberries, sprigs of mint, rose geranium or lemon verbena and the lightest dusting of confectioners' sugar. 106 calories per serving (excluding garnishes).

Variations:

Raspberry Chiffon Charlotte: Prepare exactly as directed, but substitute 1½ cups pureed and sieved ripe raspberries for the strawberries. Also substitute 1 tablespoon lemon juice for 1 of the tablespoons of orange juice. Garnish with clusters of fresh whole raspberries. 112 calories per serving.

Peach Chiffon Charlotte: Prepare as directed, but substitute 1½ cups pureed dead-ripe peaches for the strawberries (to keep peaches from darkening, mix in 1 tablespoon lemon juice). Flavor the chiffon with $\frac{1}{4}$ teaspoon almond extract. Garnish with lemon-dipped fresh peach slices and mint sprigs, artfully arranged. 106 calories per serving.

ANGEL RING À LA ALGARVE
Serves 8

It was on my first trip to Portugal some twenty years ago that I tasted this celestial dessert in the burgeoning resort of Albufeira. The idea of the dessert was so exquisite and so simple—nothing more than a meringue ring poached in a hot-water bath—that I wondered why I hadn't thought of it. That first Angel Ring was served at room temperature underneath a cloudburst of sunny apricot sauce. But I have since served it with everything from Crème Anglaise to Orange Zabaglione to fresh sliced strawberries. Take your pick.

    5 very large egg whites (at room temperature)
    ¼ teaspoon salt
    1 teaspoon lemon juice
    2 tablespoons confectioners' (10X) sugar
    ⅔ cup superfine sugar
    1 teaspoon vanilla
    ½ teaspoon almond extract

Optional Toppings (choose one; see Index for recipe page numbers):

        Orange Zabaglione Sauce (21 calories per tablespoon)
        Easy Melba Sauce (15 calories per tablespoon)
        Crème Anglaise (16 calories per tablespoon)
        Quick Cardinal Sauce (12 calories per tablespoon)
        Albufeira Apricot Sauce (10 calories per tablespoon)
        Sliced unsweetened fresh strawberries (25 calories per
          ½ cup)

Whip the egg whites with the salt and lemon juice until frothy. Add the 10X sugar and beat until silvery. Now add the superfine sugar gradually, 1 to 2 tablespoons at a time, beating hard all the while. Add the vanilla and almond extract and continue beating until the whites peak stiffly when the beater is withdrawn. Using a rubber spatula, carefully pack the meringue into an ungreased 6-cup ring mold. If the meringue is to be properly fine and feathery, you will have to work with a little bit of it at a time, packing it into the ring mold in a series of layers and pressing each into the preceding layer. Once all of the meringue is tightly packed into the mold, smooth the top as evenly as possible.

Set the ring mold in a shallow baking pan, pour water into the pan to a depth of $1\frac{1}{2}''$, then bake the meringue in the water bath in a moderately slow oven (325°F.) for about 1 hour or until pale tan on top and the ring has pulled from the sides of the mold. Remove the meringue from the oven, lift it from the water bath, set on a wire rack and cool to room temperature.

To unmold the ring, gently loosen it around the edges and around the central tube with a thin-blade spatula dipped into cold water. Invert on a round dessert plate that has been rinsed in cold water but not dried (having the plate wet means that you can center the meringue because it will slide easily on a wet plate). With paper toweling, blot up bits of moisture on the plate, then ladle several spoonfuls of the topping of your choice over the Angel Ring. Pass the remainder separately. 78 calories per serving (exclusive of topping).

RECIPE INDEX